INSTANT POT COOKBOOK

2000 Day Instant Pot Cookbook, 6 Years Instant Pot Diet Plan, the Ultimate Guide of Instant Pot cookbook

By Renee Stewart

Table of Contents

Introduction 9
Chapter 1. Everything About the Instant Pot 9
What is an Instant Pot? 9

    The instant pot will retain minerals and vitamins 9
    The instant pot cooks faster 9
    The instant pot is very easy to use 9
    The instant pot does not need anything else 10

How an Instant Pot Works(Scientific Mechanism) 10
Instant Pot Control Panel 10
Choosing a Good Instant Pot 11

    IP-DUO60 12
    IP-DUO Plus60 12
    IP-DUO50 12
    IP-DUO80 12
    IP-LUX60 V3 12
    IP-Smart Bluetooth 12

Do's and Don'ts of Instant Pot 12

    Be aware of cooking times 12
    Make sure and read all the instructions carefully 13
    Inspect your instant pot carefully 13
    Do not overfill your instant pot 13
    Do not press the timer button to set the cooking time 13
    Make sure not to add ingredients into your instant pot without the inner pot 13
    Don't use the quick release if your instant pot is overfilled or has foamy foods in it 13

Chapter 2. Beef Instant Pot Recipes 14
Cabbage Beef Soup 14
Beef & Squash Stew 14
Beef & Mixed Vegetable Stew 15
Baby Back Beef Ribs 15
Instant Pot Keto Brisket 16
Keto Thai Beef 16
Keto Beef & Tomato Stuffed Squash 17
Keto Meatloaf 17
Ginger Beef & Kale 18
Salisbury Steak 18
Keto Corned Beef 19

Beef Bourguignon 19
Beef Curry 20
Beef Stroganoff 20
Keto Beef Chili 21
Keto Chili Con Carne 21
Beef Pot Roast 22
Beef & Vegetables 22
Veal with Mushrooms 23
Beef & Kale Casserole 23

Chapter 3. Pork Instant Pot Recipes 24
Apple Cider Pork 24
Pork Sausages & Sweet Potatoes 24
Sausage & Red Beans 25
Kalua Pork 25
Pork with Hominy 26
Pork Tostadas 26
Pork Tamales 27
Pork Carnitas 27
Instant Pot Balsamic Pork Tenderloin 28
Asian Pork Short Ribs 28
Ribs & Coleslaw 29
Country-style Ribs 30
Pork Chops & Spinach Salad 31
Pork Chops & Brown Rice 31
Braised Pork 32
Chinese Barbecue Pork 32
Pork Roast with Fennel 32
Pulled Pork 33
Creamy Pork Chops 34
Pork Chops and Onion 34

Chapter 4. Lamb Instant Pot Recipes 35
Instant Pot Lamb Curry 35
Instant Pot Lamb Curry with Yogurt 35
Instant Pot Mediterranean Lamb Roast 36
Instant Pot Middle Eastern Lamb Stew 36
Instant Pot Lamb Rogan Josh 37
Instant Pot Leg of Lamb Stew with Dates & Cinnamon 37
Lavender Lamb Chops 38
Leg of Lamb & Spinach Salad 38
Lamb Shanks & Carrots 39
Lamb & Coconut Curry with Cauliflower Rice 39
Instant Pot Lamb Chops with Creamed Cauliflower 40
Instant Pot Cooked Lamb Tagine 41
Lamb, Butternut Squash & Chickpea Tagine 41
Lamb Tagine with Orange & Prunes 42

Lamb, Vegetable & Lentil Soup 42
Tuscan Lamb with White Beans 43
Moroccan Lamb Stew 43
Instant Pot Rack of Lamb 44
Garlic Rosemary Lamb 45
Lamb Shanks with Garlic & Port Wine 45

Chapter 5. Poultry Instant Pot Recipes **46**
Garlic Chicken 46
Ground Turkey & Basil Meatballs 46
Creamy Mushroom, Rosemary Chicken 47
Heavy Cream Chicken Stew 47
Ginger Spinach Chicken 48
Ginger Coconut Chicken Wings 48
Spicy, Creamy, Coconut Chicken 49
Jalapeno, Curry, Garlic Chicken Meatballs 49
Chicken Breasts & Spicy Sauce 50
Chicken & Spaghetti Squash 50
Chicken & Cauliflower Rice 50
Chicken Curry 51
Chicken and Mushrooms 52
Chicken and Salsa 52
Chicken, Walnuts, and Pomegranate 53
Turkey Instant Pot Stew 53
Lemongrass Chicken 53
Chicken and Cabbage 54
Chicken and Corn 54
Duck Chili 55
Chicken Gumbo 56
Chicken Delight 56
Party Chicken Wings 57
Roasted Chicken 57
Braised Turkey Wings 58
Braised Quail 58
Crispy Chicken 59
Chicken Salad 60
Stuffed Chicken Breasts 60
Turkey Mix and Mashed Potatoes 61

Chapter 6. Seafood Instant Pot Recipes **62**
Spicy Lemon Salmon 62
Coconut Shrimp Curry 62
Mediterranean Fish 63
Ginger, Sesame Glaze Salmon 63
Cauliflower Risotto and Salmon 64
Chili, Lime Cod 64
Instant Pot Halibut Fillets 65

Fish Fillets & Orange Sauce 65
Calamari & Tomatoes 66
Red Snapper & Chili Sauce 66
Baked Red Snapper 67
Red Snapper & Tomato Sauce 67
Thai Red Snapper 68
Lobster & Sweet Potatoes 68
Steamed Lobster 69
Simple Instant Pot Lobster 69
Spicy Sardines 70
Tasty Sardines 70
Teriyaki Salmon 71
Simple Salmon & Onion 71
Simple Instant Pot Salmon 72

Chapter 7. Soup Instant Pot Recipes 73
Sweet Potato & Broccoli Soup 73
Squash & Potato Soup 73
Parsnip Soup 73
Turkey & Carrot Soup 74
Fish Soup 74
Asparagus & Sour Cream Soup 75
Turkey & Black Bean Soup 75
Brussels Sprouts Soup 75
Chicken & Spinach Soup 76
Tomato Soup 76
Chicken Soup with Noodles 76
Creamy Sausage & Kale Soup 77
Lentils & Tomato Soup 77
Mixed Veggie Soup 78
Pork Soup 78
Sweet Potato, Carrot & Turmeric Soup 79
Creamy Bean Soup 79
Cauliflower Soup 79
Garlicky Leek & Potato Soup 80
Bean Soup with Chili 80
Chapter 8. Grain Recipes 81
Chicken & Wild Rice Soup 81
Quinoa Beef Pot 81
Keto Clam Chowder 82
Stuffed Cuttlefish 82
Saffron Chicken 83
Sesame Meatball Stew 83
Burrito with Chili Colorado 84
Sour Dumplings 85
Sausage Radish Cakes 85

Seafood Jambalaya 86
Shredded Pork Fajitas 86
Sausage Gumbo 87
Pork Fried Whole Grain Rice 87
Bacon Wrapped Jalapenos 87
Shredded Beef Tacos 88
Beef Stuffed Eggplant 88
Spicy Fire Chicken with Rice 89
Spiced Apple & Walnut Chicken 89
Pulled Chicken in Soft Whole Wheat Tacos 89
Pesto Chicken & Whole Wheat Pasta 90

Chapter 8. Egg Instant Pot Recipes 91
Eggs En Cocotte 91
Spinach & Tomato Crustless Quiche 91
Bacon & Cheese Egg Muffins 92
Meaty Crustless Quiche 92
Breakfast in a Jar 93
Bread Pudding 93
Boiled Eggs 94
Turkey Meatballs with Mushroom Gravy 94
Cheese-Stuffed Mini Turkey Meatloaves & Mushroom Gravy 95
Mushroom Stroganoff 96
Korean Style Steamed Eggs 96
Eggs De Provence 97
Instant Pot Poached Eggs Over Spicy Potato Hash 97
Instant Pot Ham & Egg Casserole 98
Instant Pot Aromatic Egg 98
Instant Pot Western Omelette Quiche 99
Instant Pot French Baked Eggs 99
Instant Pot Mexican Egg Casserole 100
Eggs Papin Poached Eggs in Bell Pepper Cup 100
Egg Bake 101

Chapter 9. Bean & Lentil Instant Pot Recipes 102
Mung Bean Dahl 102
Red Bean & Lentil Chili 102
Falafel 103
Chickpea Curry 103
Lentil Sloppy Joe's 104
Lentil and Wild Rice Pilaf 104
Instant Pot Hummus 105
Stewed Chickpeas 105
Rainbow Beans 106
Northern White Bean Dip 106
Greek-Style Gigantes Beans with Feta 107
Chili Con Carne 107

Smokey Sweet Black-Eyed Peas & Greens 108
Tex Mex Pinto Beans 108
Instant Pot Charros 109
Three Bean Salad 109
Beans Stew 110
Not Re-Fried Beans 111
Baked Beans 111
Stewed Tomatoes & Green Beans 112

Chapter 10. Vegetable Instant Pot Recipes 113
Sweet Potato, Red Lentil, Hemp Burgers 113
Creamy Kidney Beans & Lentils 113
Sweet Potato, Lentil & Coconut Curry 114
Millet & Lentils with Vegetables & Mushrooms 114
Basmati Rice 115
Vegan Butter Chickpeas 115
Potatoes & Peas 116
Spicy Veggie Mix 116
Vegetable Masala Mix 117
Masala Eggplant 117
Mushroom Matar Masala 118
Curried Potato Eggplant 118
Coconut Tofu Curry 119
Tomato Stewed Green Bean 119
Sesame Tofu 120
Lentil & Spinach Dal 120
Spinach Chana Masala 121
Lentil Bolognese 122
Coconut Quinoa Curry 122
Garlic Mashed Potatoes 122
Marinara Sauce 123
Cauliflower Rice 123
Delicious Dumplings 124
Sweet Potato Pie 124
Tasty Tofu 125
Instant Pot Broccoli & Tomato Pasta 125
Refried Beans 126
Peanut & Sweet Potato Stew 126
White Bean Stew with Kale & Winter Squash 127
Lasagna Soup 127

Chapter 11. Desserts & Appetizer Instant Pot Recipes 129
Chocolate Almond Fudge Cake 129
Pumpkin Chocolate Chip Bundt Cake 129
Tapioca Pudding 130
Carrot Cake 130
Brownies 131

Apple Crisp 131
Vanilla Fruit Cake 131
Creamy Chocolate Cheesecake 132
Apple Crumb Cake 133
Raspberry Cream Cheesecake 133
Crema Catalana 134
Cranberry Cake 135
Chocoflan 136
Cheese Flan Cake 137
Raspberry Curd 137
Fruit Clafoutis Cake 138
Yams Citrus 138
Chocolate Custard 139
Bread Pudding 139
Blueberry Custard 140
Purple Pudding 140
Mango & Cashew Cake 141
Corn Pudding 141
Pumpkin Pie 141
Instant Pot Chocolate Fondue 142
Conclusion **143**

Introduction

Chapter 1. Everything About the Instant Pot

What is an Instant Pot?

The Instant Pot is a wonderful kitchen aide, it is a multi-cooker which was designed to prepare various meals quickly and deliciously. Using an Instant Pot, you will be able to slow cook, pressure cook, sauté, make rice, yogurt and much more, all of these can be done just by pressing a few buttons and letting your instant pot do the rest. Most models come with an automatic shut-off button, so your food will not overcook once it is ready. There is plenty of benefits connected to the instant pot, including:

The instant pot will retain minerals and vitamins

Pressure cooking will allow you to retain more minerals and vitamins, opposed to other cooking methods such as steaming or boiling. The longer you cook your foods, the more nutrition will be lost out of your food, especially when cooking vegetables. Using the instant pot that only takes minutes to cook, it will retain most of its minerals and vitamins needed to help fuel your body. Pressure cooking can also make foods easier to digest, such as lentils and beans. In a word, cook foods in your instant pot without worrying about upsetting your stomach.

The instant pot cooks faster

With an instant pot it uses pressure and heat to cook your foods; it will take much less time to cook foods. If for example it takes you one hour to cook chicken in a conventional oven it may only take 20 minutes or less to do the same job with your instant pot.

The instant pot is very easy to use

When you are preparing your meals using the conventional oven or stovetop you need to pay full attention to make sure you do not burn or ruin your meal. With the instant pot you just need to place the ingredients into it and allow it to do the rest. No need any cooking skills, no need to stand before it when cooking. The instant pot is also very easy to clean. All you have to do is to remove the gasket from the cover and wash it with warm water.

The instant pot does not need anything else

The only kitchen appliance you will need is the instant pot. You can prepare breakfast, lunch, dinner and dessert, all with the instant pot. In this cookbook you will have 500 easy and delicious instant pot recipes to try out!

How an Instant Pot Works (Scientific Mechanism)

The instant pot is a great kitchen appliance to help you to prepare meals through pressure cooking. With pressure cooking steam is used and sealed in the pressure cooker, it is an airtight cooking pot. If you add some water, the pressure will trap the vapor that rises from the liquid. Thus, it causes the pressure to raise within the cooker, along with the temperature of the water. With the increased temperature in both water and pressure, cooking time is accelerated.

The instant pot is easy to use, all you have to do is to add your ingredients into the pot and adjust the settings. You will learn what and how to use the various buttons on your instant pot.

Instant Pot Control Panel

Below is an explanation about the different controls and settings on the instant pot:

Manual: This is the main button on your instant pot. With this button you can manually set the pressure and cooking time.

Keep Warm/Cancel: This button will cancel any functions and will turn your instant pot off. If your cooking is completed, the instant pot will automatically enter the *keep warm* mode and will stay there for 10 hours. You can cancel the function at any time.

Pressure: When you cook in manual button, this button will adjust your settings of pressure to low, medium, or high.

Slow Cook: By pressing this button you will turn your instant pot into a slow cooker.

Timer: This is the button you would use for delayed cooking. You first would select a cooking function and make any required adjustments. Then you can adjust the timer button using the +/- buttons.
Sauté: With this button it will allow you to sauté and brown your foods. When you are cooking using this button you will have the lid off, this will enable you to stir your ingredients. You can adjust the heat from sauté by pressing the normal setting, more, or less. Normal is for regular browning, more is for stir-frying, and less is for simmering.
Meat/Stew: With this button you can set your instant pot to high pressure for 35 minutes.
Poultry: This button will automatically set your instant pot to high pressure for 15 minutes.
Steam: This button will automatically place your instant pot on high for 10 minutes.
Porridge: This button will automatically set your instant pot to high pressure for 20 minutes.
Multi-Grain: This button will automatically set your instant pot at high pressure for 40 minutes.
Bean/Chili: This button will automatically set your instant pot to high pressure for 30 minutes.
Soup: This button automatically will set your instant pot to high pressure for 30 minutes.
Yogurt: Pressing this button will allow you to make yogurt using your instant pot.
You need to know how to release pressure with a pressure cooker. With the instant pot there are two ways either through natural release or quick release. Using the natural release allows the pressure to release on it own naturally. With the quick release you turn the valve on top from the 'sealing' setting to the 'venting' setting.

Choosing a Good Instant Pot

There are diverse types of instant pots available on the market. You will have to decide which is the best one for you and your needs. One of the most popular is a 6-quart version to larger and more advanced models. Below are some options you might want to consider when choosing your instant pot:

IP-DUO60
This model of instant pot is the most popular. It offers a 7-in-1 multifunctional countertop appliance; which combines a slow cooker, pressure cooker, rice cooker, yogurt maker, steamer, sauté/browning functionality and a warmer.

IP-DUO Plus60
This model is an upgrade to the regular IP-DUO60. This upgraded version includes settings such as Egg, Cake, and Sterilize buttons. The alarm clock on this model is a blue LCD screen. The inner bowl also offers more comprehensive max/min fill lines.

IP-DUO50
This model of instant pot holds five quarts.

IP-DUO80
This model of instant pot has a capacity of eight quarts. It is more expensive than others, but the extra space might be useful.

IP-LUX60 V3
This model of instant pot has egg and cake settings on the control panel. However, it does not have poultry, yogurt or beans/chili settings, nor an option to cook on low pressure. It also does not come with some of the accessories that other models have.

IP-Smart Bluetooth
This model of instant pot holds six quarts with all the basic functions, and can connect via Bluetooth to your phone; so, you are able to program and monitor cooking from anywhere using the Instant Pot Smart Cooker App.
Choosing the right instant pot for yourself should not be too complicated. It is best to purchase new appliances not used, as they could have broken buttons and complications.

Do's and Don'ts of Instant Pot

If you are new to using an instant pot it would be a clever idea to become familiar with what you should and should not do with your instant pot. Below are some helpful tips for cooking with an instant pot:

Be aware of cooking times
Cooking times are a great indicator to give you an idea when your food should be cooked, but the actual cooking time can vary. This is largely due to different

ingredients being used and done in different situations. For instance, different meats will take different amounts of time to soften up. Make sure to be mindful of your cooking by inspecting the result to make sure it is cooked through. You can test a small piece from your meal that you are preparing to see that it is cooked through before removing it from the instant pot.

Make sure and read all the instructions carefully
When you get your new instant pot, read all the instructions carefully to avoid any mishaps or damaging your instant pot.

Inspect your instant pot carefully
To keep your instant pot as a reliable appliance you need to make sure that you keep it clean. If parts on your instant pot begin to wear out then they need to be replaced by original parts, or you could run the risk of permanently damaging your instant pot.

Do not overfill your instant pot
If you fill your instant pot with too much food and liquid this could cause the venting knob to become clogged. There is a max line on the inner pot make sure that you do not go past this, so you won't overfill your instant pot.

Do not press the timer button to set the cooking time
People often mistake the 'timer' button for the button to set the cook time, and then wonder why their instant pot is not working. Make sure to check that the 'timer' button is not lit before you leave.

Make sure not to add ingredients into your instant pot without the inner pot
You do not want to pour ingredients into your instant pot without its inner pot being in place, believe me this happens a lot. This can cause damage and will be time consuming to clean.

Don't use the quick release if your instant pot is overfilled or has foamy foods in it
Inexperienced users of instant pots often get the Quick Pressure Release and Natural Pressure Release confused. If you use the Quick Release when you are cooking foamy foods, such as applesauce, beans, or grains, it could splatter everywhere. To prevent this from occurring use the natural release or release the pressure gradually.

Chapter 2. Beef Instant Pot Recipes

Cabbage Beef Soup
Cook Time: 40 minutes　　　　　　　　*Servings: 6*
Ingredients:
- 1 head green cabbage, chopped
- 1 lb. lean ground beef
- 1 head red cabbage, chopped
- 1 can (28-ounce) tomatoes, diced
- 1 celery stalk, chopped
- 3 cups water
- 1 teaspoon fresh ground black pepper
- 1 teaspoon salt
- 1 tablespoon fresh parsley, chopped

Directions:
First press the sauté button on your instant pot. Add in the ground beef. Sauté your beef until it is no longer pink; drain. Press the keep warm/cancel setting to stop sauté mode. Return your ground beef to your instant pot. Add in the cabbage, diced tomatoes, celery, parsley, water, salt and pepper. Stir well. Close and seal the lid. Press the meat/stew button. Cook on high pressure for 20 minutes. Once completed the instant pot will automatically switch to 'keep warm' mode. Allow it to 'keep warm' mode for 10 minutes. Use the 'quick-release' when done. Open the lid carefully. Stir the ingredients, serve and garnish with fresh parsley.

Nutritional Information per serving:
Calories: 115　Fat: 4.4g　Carbohydrates: 11g　Dietary Fiber: 3g　Protein: 11g

Beef & Squash Stew
Cook Time: 50 minutes　　　　　　　　*Servings: 4*
Ingredients:
- 2 lbs. butternut squash, peeled, chopped into chunks
- 1 lb. lean ground beef
- 1 (6-ounce) can sliced mushrooms
- 2 garlic cloves
- 1 red onion, diced
- 4 cups beef broth
- 2 tablespoons butter
- 1 teaspoon fresh rosemary, chopped
- 1 teaspoon black pepper
- 1 teaspoon salt
- 2 teaspoons paprika

Directions:
Press the sauté button on your instant pot. Melt the butter. Sauté the garlic and onions for 1 minute. Add the ground beef, mushrooms, and butternut squash. Sauté until the beef is no longer pink and the vegetables have softened. Press the keep warm/cancel button to stop the sauté mode. Add in beef stock, paprika, salt, black pepper and rosemary, mix well. Close and seal the lid. Press the soup button. Cook on high pressure for 30 minutes. After the 30 minutes is up your instant pot will automatically switch to the 'keep warm' mode and remain in 'keep warm' for 10 minutes. Use the 'quick-release' when done and open the lid carefully, stir ingredients and serve.

Nutritional Information per serving:
Calories: 245　Fat: 7g　Protein: 25g　Carbohydrates: 15g　Dietary Fiber: 8g

Beef & Mixed Vegetable Stew

Cook Time: 45 minutes **Servings: 4**
Ingredients:
- 4 zucchinis, chopped
- 1 ½ lbs. stewing beef chunks
- 4 cups vegetable broth
- 2 cups frozen peas
- 2 carrots, chopped
- 1 tablespoon coconut oil
- ½ cup ghee
- 4 cloves garlic, minced
- 1 red onion, chopped
- 2 tomatoes, chopped
- 1 tablespoon ginger
- 2 tablespoons cumin
- Salt and pepper to taste

Directions:
Press the sauté button on instant pot. Heat your coconut oil. Add onions and garlic and sweat for 1 minute. Add in your stewing beef and brown all sides. Add the zucchini, peas and carrots. Press the keep warm/cancel setting to stop the sauté mode. Add your ghee and stir well. Now add the vegetable stock, tomatoes, ginger, cumin, salt and pepper. Stir well. Close and seal lid of pot and press the meat/stew button. Cook for 35 minutes. When your instant pot timer beeps, quick-release or naturally release pressure. Open the pot lid carefully. Stir and spoon into serving bowls.

Nutritional Information per serving:
Calories: 200   Protein: 31g   Fat: 40g   Carbohydrates: 13g   Dietary Fiber: 4g

Baby Back Beef Ribs

Cook Time: 45 minutes **Servings: 4**
Ingredients:
- 1 rack of baby back beef ribs
- 2 cups beef broth
- 2 tablespoons granulated Splenda
- 2 tablespoons soy sauce
- 2 tablespoons coconut oil
- 4 garlic cloves, minced
- 3 tablespoons ginger, grated
- 1 teaspoon onion powder
- 1 teaspoon cayenne pepper
- 1 teaspoon low-carb brown sugar
- 1 teaspoon ground mustard
- 1 tablespoon paprika
- 1 tablespoon chili powder
- Salt and pepper to taste

Directions:
In a small bowl mix together chili powder, ginger, ground mustard, paprika, cayenne pepper, onion powder, salt and pepper and stir well. Add in brown sugar and Splenda. Rinse your ribs, you will want the ribs to be a bit damp, so the seasoning will cling to them. Rub seasoning mix on both sides of ribs. Place the ribs on a flat baking sheet. Preheat your oven to broil. Place the baking sheet under the broiler for 5 minutes per side. Press the sauté mode on your instant pot. Heat the coconut oil. Add ginger and garlic. Cook for 1 minute. Add soy sauce and beef broth. Boil for 15 seconds. Stir well. Press keep warm/cancel setting to end the sauté mode. Slice the rack of ribs up into chunks of 4-5 ribs and place them into

your instant pot. Close and seal the lid and press manual button. Cook on high-pressure for 35 minutes. When done release the pressure quickly or naturally. Open lid carefully and serve.

Nutritional Information per serving:
Calories: 500   Fat: 40g   Carbohydrates: 1.5g   Dietary Fiber: 0.9g   Protein: 55g

---

Instant Pot Keto Brisket
Cook Time: 50 minutes   *Servings: 5*
Ingredients:

- 2 lbs. of beef brisket
- 2 tablespoons coconut oil
- 2 shallots, thinly sliced
- 3 tablespoons tomato paste
- 1 tablespoon dry mustard
- 2 tablespoons Worcestershire sauce
- 2 tablespoons soy sauce
- 8-ounces low-carb beer
- Salt and pepper to taste

Directions:
Add all the ingredients to a large Ziploc bag and massage the ingredients. Allow them to marinate for 2 hours. When ready to cook, transfer the ingredients into your instant pot. Close the lid and press the manual setting. Cook on high-pressure for 40 minutes. Once done, quick-release or naturally release the pressure. Open the instant pot lid carefully. Press the sauté mode. Cook until all the liquids evaporate. Remove the brisket. Let rest for 15 minutes before slicing. Serve and enjoy!

Nutritional Information per serving:
Calories: 400   Fat: 20g   Carbohydrates: 3.5g   Dietary Fiber: 0.5g   Protein: 45g

---

Keto Thai Beef
Cook Time: 30 minutes   *Servings: 6*
Ingredients:

- 1 lb. of beef, cut into strips
- 2 tablespoons coconut oil
- 4 garlic cloves, minced
- 2 teaspoons ginger, grated
- 2 cups beef broth
- Zest and juice of 1 lemon
- 1 red bell pepper, chopped
- 1 green bell pepper, chopped
- 1 tablespoon coconut amino
- 1 cup roasted pecans
- Salt and pepper to taste

Directions:
Press the sauté button on your instant pot. Heat the coconut oil. Sauté ginger and garlic for 1 minute. Add in the beef strips. Sear them for 2 minutes per side. Add bell peppers, salt and pepper. Continue to cook until meat is no longer pink. Add the coconut amino, zest and juice of lemon, pecans, and beef broth. Stir well. Close and seal lid. Press the manual setting and cook on high-pressure for 15 minutes. When done, naturally release the pressure. Open lid carefully and let sit for 10 minutes. Serve.

Keto Beef & Tomato Stuffed Squash
Cook Time: 30 minutes   **Servings: 4**

Ingredients:
- 1 lb. of beef chopped into chunks
- 1 yellow bell pepper
- 1 green bell pepper
- 2 tablespoons ghee, melted
- 2 tablespoons coconut oil
- 1 lb. butternut squash, peeled and chopped
- 2 (14-ounce) cans of diced tomatoes
- 4 garlic cloves, minced
- 1 teaspoon cayenne pepper
- 2 tablespoons fresh parsley, chopped
- 1 tablespoon fresh rosemary, chopped
- 1 tablespoon fresh thyme, chopped
- 1 yellow or red onion, chopped
- Salt and pepper to taste

Directions:
Press sauté button on your instant pot. Heat the coconut oil. Add the onion and garlic and sweat for 2 minutes. Add the beef chunks, bell peppers, and butternut squash. Sauté until the meat is no longer pink and veggies have softened. Press keep warm/cancel to end the sauté mode. Add in the melted ghee, tomatoes, parsley, rosemary, cayenne, salt and pepper. Stir well. Close the lid and seal. Press the manual button and cook on high-pressure for 20 minutes. Quick-release the pressure when done and open lid carefully. Serve.

Nutritional Information per serving:
Calories: 250   Fat: 7g   Dietary Fiber: 2g   Carbohydrates: 4g   Protein: 10g

Keto Meatloaf
Cook Time: 35 minutes   **Servings: 4**

Ingredients:
- 3 lbs. lean ground beef
- 4 garlic cloves, minced
- 1 yellow onion, chopped
- 1 cup mushrooms, chopped
- 3 large eggs
- ¼ cup parsley, fresh, chopped
- ¼ cup mozzarella cheese, grated
- ¼ cup parmesan cheese, grated
- ½ cup almond flour
- 2 cups water
- 2 tablespoons coconut oil
- 2 tablespoons sugar-free ketchup
- Salt and pepper to taste

Instructions:
Cover trivet with aluminum foil. In a large bowl, add ingredients (excluding the water) until well combined. Form into a meatloaf. Pour water in your instant pot. Place trivet inside. Place the meatloaf on trivet. Close and seal lid. Press manual button and cook on high-pressure for 25 minutes. When done, natural release the pressure. Allow meatloaf to rest for 5 minutes before slicing. Serve.

Nutritional Information per serving:
Calories: 250   Fat: 15g   Dietary Fiber: 3g   Carbohydrates: 5g   Protein: 25g

Ginger Beef & Kale
Cook Time: 35 minutes **Servings: 4**
Ingredients:
- 1 lb. beef cut into chunks
- 1 bunch of kale, stemmed, chopped
- 2 tablespoons coconut oil
- 2 tablespoons ginger, fresh, grated
- 4 garlic cloves, minced
- 1 red onion, chopped
- 2 cups beef broth
- 1 teaspoon paprika
- ½ lb. mushrooms, sliced
- Salt and pepper to taste
- Sesame seeds for garnish
- 2 spring onions, chopped, for garnish

Directions:
Press sauté button on your instant pot. Heat your coconut oil. Add in the onions and garlic and sweat for 1 minute. Add the beef chunks and sauté until the meat is no longer pink. Press the keep warm/cancel setting to end the sauté mode. Add in the remaining ingredients. Stir well. Close and seal the lid. Press manual button and cook at high-pressure for 25 minutes. When the timer beeps, quick-release or naturally release pressure. Open the lid and stir ingredients. Divide into serving plates, garnish with sesame seeds and chopped spring onion. Serve.

Nutritional Information per serving:
Calories: 325   Fat: 15g   Carbohydrates: 20g   Dietary Fiber: 2.5g   Protein: 30g

Salisbury Steak
Cook Time: 35 minutes **Servings: 4**
Ingredients:
- 2 lbs. lean ground beef
- 1 tablespoon coconut oil
- ½ yellow onion, diced
- 1 tablespoon Worcestershire sauce
- ¼ cup beef broth
- ¼ cup coconut flour
- 1 egg
- 1 tablespoon bread crumbs
- 2 garlic cloves, minced
- 1 tablespoon parsley, fresh, chopped
- Salt and pepper to taste

Gravy Ingredients:
- 2 cups mushrooms, sliced
- 2 tablespoons ghee, melted
- 1 onion, sliced
- 2 tablespoons parsley, fresh, chopped
- ¼ cup sour cream
- 1 tablespoon tomato paste
- 1 teaspoon Worcestershire sauce
- Salt and pepper to taste

Directions:
In a large mixing bowl, steak ingredients, except coconut oil. Shape into round patties, ¼ inch thick. Set aside. Press your sauté button on your instant pot. Heat the coconut oil. Cook the patties 2 minutes per side, until they are golden brown. Remove the patties and set aside. Heat the ghee and add gravy ingredients. Stir well. Press the keep warm/cancel button to end sauté mode. Return patties to your instant pot. Close and seal the lid. Press

manual switch and cook at high-pressure for 25 minutes. When done quick-release pressure. Open lid carefully. Serve.
Nutritional Information per serving:
Calories: 425   Fat: 35g   Carbohydrates: 5g   Protein: 32g   Dietary Fiber: 1g

---

Keto Corned Beef
Cook Time: 60 minutes   **Servings: 6**
Ingredients:
- 4 lbs. beef brisket
- 2 oranges, sliced
- 2 garlic cloves, minced
- 3 bay leaves
- 1 tablespoon dried dill
- 11 ounces celery, sliced thin
- 2 yellow onions, sliced thin
- 4 cinnamon sticks, cut in half
- 17 ounces of water
- Salt and pepper to taste

Directions:
Place your beef in a bowl, and cover with some water, set aside to soak for a few hours, drain and transfer to your instant pot. Add in orange slices, celery, bay leaves, onions, garlic, dill, cinnamon, salt and pepper. Stir and cover instant pot and cook on the meat/stew setting for 50 minutes. Release using quick-release or natural release of pressure, set the beef aside for 5 minutes. Transfer meat to cutting board, slice and place onto serving plates. Drizzle the juice and vegetables from instant pot over the beef. Serve.
Nutritional Information per serving:
Calories: 251   Fat: 3.14g   Fiber: 1g   Carbs: 11g   Protein: 17g

---

Beef Bourguignon
Cook Time: 30 minutes
Servings: 6
Ingredients:
- 10 lbs. round steak, cut into small cubes
- 2 tablespoons white flour
- 8 ounces mushrooms, cut into quarters
- 3 bacon slices, chopped
- 1 cup dry red wine
- ½ cup beef stock
- 2 carrots, peeled and sliced
- 12 pearl onions
- 2 garlic cloves, minced
- ¼ teaspoon basil, dried
- Salt and pepper to taste

Directions:
Set the instant pot on sauté mode, add the bacon, and brown it for two minutes. Add the beef pieces, stir and brown for 5 minutes. Add the flour and stir. Add wine, basil, garlic, onions, salt and pepper, cover and cook on the meat/stew setting for 20 minutes. Release the pressure, naturally, uncover the instant pot and add in the mushrooms and carrots. Cover the instant pot again and cook on manual setting for 5 minutes. Release the pressure again naturally, divide the beef bourguignon among serving plates. Serve.
Nutritional Information per serving:
Calories: 442   Fat: 17.2g   Fiber: 3g   Carbs: 16g   Protein: 39g

Beef Curry
Cook Time: 20 minutes
Servings: 4
Ingredients:
- 2 lbs. beef steak, cubed
- 3 potatoes, diced
- 2 tablespoons virgin olive oil
- 1 tablespoon Dijon mustard
- 2 garlic cloves, minced
- 2 yellow onions, chopped
- 2 ½ tablespoons curry powder
- 10 ounces canned coconut milk
- 2 tablespoons tomato sauce
- Salt and pepper to taste

Directions:
Set your instant pot to sauté mode, add oil, and heat. Add the garlic and onions and cook for 4 minutes. Add the potatoes and mustard, stir, cook for 1 minute. Add the beef and brown on all sides. Add the curry powder, salt and pepper and cook for 2 minutes. Add the coconut milk and tomato sauce, stir and cover your instant pot. Cook on the meat/stew setting for 10 minutes. Release the pressure with quick-release and then uncover pot. Divide the curry onto serving plates. Serve.

Nutritional Information per serving:
Calories: 434   Fat: 20g   Fiber: 2.9g   Carbs: 14g   Protein: 27.5g

Beef Stroganoff
Cook Time: 25 minutes
Servings: 4
Ingredients:
- 10 lbs. beef, cut into small cubes
- 2 ½ tablespoons almond flour
- 2 garlic cloves, minced
- 2 ½ tablespoons olive oil
- 4 ounces mushrooms, sliced
- 1 ½ tablespoon tomato paste
- 3 tablespoons Worcestershire sauce
- 13 ounces beef stock
- 8 ounces sour cream
- Egg noodles, already cooked, for serving
- Salt and pepper to taste

Directions:
Put all the beef, flour, salt and pepper in a bowl and toss to coat. Set your instant pot on sauté mode, add olive oil, and heat. Add in the meat and brown on all sides. Add the garlic, mushrooms, onion, Worcestershire sauce, stock and tomato paste and mix well. Cover instant pot and cook on the meat/stew setting for 20 minutes. Use quick-release to release the pressure. Remove the top of pot and add in the sour cream, salt and pepper. Divide among serving plates. Serve.

Nutritional Information per serving:
Calories: 335   Fat: 18.4g   Fiber: 1.3g   Carbs: 22.5g   Protein: 20.1g

Keto Beef Chili
Cook Time: 40 minutes
Servings: 6
Ingredients:
- 1 ½ lbs. ground beef
- 17 ounces beef stock
- 16 ounces mixed beans, soaked overnight and drained
- 1 sweet onion, chopped
- 28 ounces canned diced tomatoes
- 6 garlic cloves, chopped
- 1 teaspoon chili powder
- 1 bay leaf
- 3 tablespoons chili powder
- 4 carrots, chopped
- 2 tablespoons olive oil
- 7 jalapeno peppers, diced

Directions:
Set your instant pot on sauté mode and add half of the olive oil and heat it up. Add in the beef and brown for 8 minutes, then transfer to a bowl. Add the rest of the oil to the instant pot and heat up. Add in the jalapenos, onion, carrots and garlic, stir and sauté for 4 minutes. Add tomatoes and stir. Add beans, stock, chili powder, bay leaf, beef, salt and pepper. Cover and cook on the bean/chilli setting for 25 minutes. Release the pressure naturally, uncover your instant pot, stir chili and transfer into serving bowls. Serve.

Nutritional Information per serving:
Calories: 272   Fat: 5g   Fiber: 1g   Carbs: 32g   Protein: 25g

Keto Chili Con Carne
Cook Time: 30 minutes
Servings: 4
Ingredients:
- 1 lb. of ground beef
- 4 tablespoons coconut oil
- 1 yellow onion, chopped
- 2 garlic cloves, minced
- 4 ounces kidney beans, soaked overnight and drained
- 8 ounces tomatoes, canned, diced
- 1 tablespoon chili powder
- ½ teaspoon cumin
- 5 ounces water
- 1 teaspoon tomato paste

Directions:
Set your instant pot to sauté mode, add 1 tablespoon coconut oil and heat it up. Add in the meat and brown for a few minutes then transfer to a bowl. Add the rest of the coconut oil to the instant pot and heat it up. Add in the garlic, and onion and cook for 3 minutes. Return the beef to pot, beans, tomato paste, chili powder, tomatoes, cumin, salt, pepper and water. Cover pot and cook on the bean/chili setting for 18 minutes. Release the pressure naturally. Uncover the instant pot and divide the chili into serving bowls. Serve.

Nutritional Information per serving:
Calories: 256   Fat: 8g   Fiber: 1g   Carbs: 22g   Protein: 35g

Beef Pot Roast
Cook Time: 1 hour
Servings: 6
Ingredients:
- 3 lbs. beef roast
- 17 ounces beef stock
- 3 ounces red wine
- 1 yellow onion, chopped
- 4 garlic cloves, minced
- 3 carrots, chopped
- 5 potatoes, chopped
- ½ teaspoon smoked paprika
- Salt and pepper to taste

Directions:
In a bowl mix the salt, pepper and paprika and rub on beef and place it into the instant pot. Add the garlic, stock, wine, onion, and toss to coat. Cover the instant pot and cook on meat/stew setting for 50 minutes. Release the pressure naturally. Uncover the instant pot and add in the potatoes and carrots and cover it again. Cook on the steam setting for 10 minutes. Release the pressure naturally again, uncover and transfer the roast to a serving platter. Drizzle roast with cooking juices and serve with the veggies on the side.

Nutritional Information per serving:
Calories: 290   Fat: 20g   Fiber: 1g   Carbs: 2g   Protein: 35g

Beef & Vegetables
Cook Time: 30 minutes
Servings: 4
Ingredients:
- 1 ½ lbs. beef chuck roast, cubed
- 2 tablespoons of coconut oil
- 4 tablespoons almond flour
- 1 yellow onion, chopped
- 2 cups water
- 2 garlic cloves, minced
- 2 tablespoons red wine
- ½ bunch parsley, chopped
- 4 potatoes, chopped
- 2 carrots, chopped
- 2 celery stalks, chopped
- ½ teaspoon thyme, dried
- 2 cups beef stock
- Salt and pepper to taste

Directions:
Mix the salt and pepper with half of almond flour and season the beef with it. Set the instant pot on sauté mode, add the coconut oil and heat it up. Add the beef and brown it for 2 minutes. Once meat is browned transfer to bowl. Add the onion to the instant pot and cook for 3 minutes. Add the garlic, stir and cook for 1 minute. Add the wine, stir and cook for 15 seconds. Add the rest of the almond flour and stir for 2 minutes.

Return the meat to the instant pot, add water, thyme, stock and cover and cook on meat/stew setting for 12 minutes. Release the pressure naturally. Remove the lid of instant pot and add potatoes and carrots into pot. Cover pot and cook on steam setting for 5 minutes. Release the pressure naturally. Uncover the instant pot, divide among serving plates, serve with parsley sprinkled on top.

Nutritional Information per serving:
Calories: 221   Fat: 5.3g   Fiber: 1g   Carbs: 20.2g   Protein: 32.7g

Veal with Mushrooms
Cook Time: 35 minutes **Servings:** 4
Ingredients:
- 3.5 ounces button mushrooms, sliced
- 3.5 ounces shiitake mushrooms, sliced
- 9 ounces beef stock
- 16 ounces shallots, chopped
- 17 ounces potatoes, chopped
- 2 lbs. veal shoulder, cut into medium chunks
- 3 ½ tablespoons coconut oil
- 1/8 teaspoon thyme, dried
- 1 teaspoon sage, dried
- 2 tablespoons chives, chopped
- 2 garlic cloves, minced
- 1 tablespoon almond flour
- 2 ounces white wine
- Salt and pepper to taste

Directions:
Set your instant pot to sautė mode and add 1 1/2 tablespoons of coconut oil and heat it up. Add the veal, season with salt and pepper, brown for 5 minutes and transfer to bowl. Add the rest of coconut oil into instant pot and heat it up. Add the mushrooms and stir and cook for 3 minutes. Add the garlic and cook for 1 minute, transfer to bowl.
Add the almond flour and wine to the instant pot and cook for 1 minute. Add the stock, thyme and sage to instant pot and return the meat to pot. Stir, cover and cook on the meat/stew setting for 20 minutes. Release the pressure naturally. Uncover the pot, return the garlic and mushrooms, add the potatoes, shallots stir and cover. Cook on the manual setting for 4 minutes. Release the pressure again and uncover the pot, add salt and pepper, chives and stir. Divide among serving bowls. Serve.

Nutritional Information per serving:
Calories: 395   Fat: 18g   Fiber: 1.4g   Carbs: 7.1g   Protein: 47.8g

Beef & Kale Casserole
Cook Time: 20 minutes **Servings:** 4
Ingredients:
- 2 cups of kale, fresh, chopped
- 1 lb. ground beef
- 13 ounces mozzarella cheese, shredded
- 16 ounces tomato puree
- 1 celery stalk
- 1 carrot, chopped
- 1 yellow onion, chopped
- 2 tablespoons butter
- 1 tablespoons red wine
- Salt and pepper to taste

Directions:
Set your instant pot on sautė mode, add the butter and melt it. Add the onion, carrot, stir and cook for 5 minutes. Add the beef, salt, pepper and cook for 10 minutes. Add the wine and stir and cook for 1 minute. Add the kale, tomato puree, cover with water and stir set on manual setting for 6 minutes. Release the pressure naturally. Uncover the pot and add the cheese and stir. Divide into serving bowls. Serve.

Nutritional Information per serving:
Calories: 182   Fat: 11g   Fiber: 1.4g   Carbs: 31g   Protein: 22g

Chapter 3. Pork Instant Pot Recipes

Apple Cider Pork
Cook Time: 25 minutes **Servings: 4**
Ingredients:
- 2lbs. pork loin
- 2 tablespoons extra virgin olive oil
- 2 cups apple cider
- 1 yellow onion, peeled, chopped
- 1 tablespoon onion flakes, dried
- 2 apples, cored and chopped
- Salt and pepper to taste

Directions:
Set your instant pot on the sauté mode, add the oil, and heat it up. Add the pork, dried onion, salt, pepper, and stir. Brown the meat on all sides and transfer to a plate. Add the onion to the instant pot, stir and cook for 2 minutes. Add cider, apples, salt and pepper, and return the meat to the instant pot. Stir. Cover and cook on Manual mode for 20 minutes. Release the pressure naturally, and uncover the instant pot. Transfer pork to cutting board, slice and divide amongst serving dishes. Add the sauce and mix from instant pot. Serve.

Nutritional Information per serving:
Calories: 450   Fat: 22g   Fiber: 2.2g   Carbs: 29g   Protein: 37.2g

Pork Sausages & Sweet Potatoes
Cook Time: 15 minutes **Servings: 6**
Ingredients:
For the sweet potatoes:
- 4 sweet potatoes, peeled and cut into cubes
- 1 teaspoon dry mustard
- Salt and pepper to taste
- 1 tablespoon butter
- 4-ounces milk, warmed
- 6-ounces water

For the sausages:
- 6 pork sausages
- 1 tablespoon of cornstarch mixed with one tablespoon water
- Salt and pepper to taste
- 3-ounces water
- 3-ounces red wine
- ½ cup onion jam
- 2 tablespoons extra virgin olive oil

Directions:
Place the sweet potatoes into the instant pot, add 6-ounces water, salt, pepper, stir and cover, and cook on steam mode for 5 minutes. Release the pressure with quick-release. Drain the sweet potatoes and place them in a bowl. Add the milk and butter, mustard, more salt and pepper and mash them well. Set the dish aside.

Set your instant pot to sauté mode, add the oil and heat it up. Add the sausages and brown them on all sides. Add the onion jam, wine, 3-ounces of water, salt and pepper. Cover the instant pot and cook on the meat/stew setting for 8 minutes. Release the pressure with quick-release and divide the sausages among serving plates. Add cornstarch to mixture in instant pot and stir well. Drizzle the sauce from instant pot over the sausages and serve with mashed sweet potatoes.

Nutritional Information per serving:
Calories: 435   Fat: 33g   Fiber: 15g   Carbs: 44.2g   Protein: 55g

---

Sausage & Red Beans
Cooking Time: 30 minutes
Servings: 8
Ingredients:

- 1 lb. smoked sausage, sliced
- 1 bay leaf
- 1 lb. red beans, dried, soaked overnight and drained
- 2 tablespoons Cajun seasoning
- 1 celery stalk, chopped
- Salt and pepper to taste
- ½ green bell pepper, seeded, chopped
- 1 small yellow onion, peeled, chopped
- 1 garlic clove, peeled, chopped
- ¼ teaspoon cumin
- 5 cups water
- 1 teaspoon parsley, dried

Directions:
In your instant pot mix the beans, bay leaf, sausage, Cajun seasoning, celery, salt, bell pepper, parsley, cumin, garlic, onion, pepper, water and stir. Cover and cook on Bean/Chili setting for 30 minutes. Release the pressure using quick-release, uncover the instant pot, divide and mix into serving bowls. Serve.

Nutritional Information per serving:
Calories: 248   Fat: 15g   Fiber: 12.3g   Carbs: 40g   Protein: 29g

---

Kalua Pork
Cooking Time: 90 minutes
Servings: 5
Ingredients:

- 4 lbs. pork shoulder, cut into half
- ½ cup water
- 1 tablespoon liquid smoke
- 2 tablespoons coconut oil
- Salt and pepper to taste
- Steamed green beans, for serving

Directions:
Set your instant pot on the sauté mode, add the oil and heat it up. Add in the pork, salt and pepper. Brown the meat for 3 minutes on each side. Transfer meat to a plate. Add the water and liquid smoke to the instant pot and stir. Return the meat to the instant pot and stir ingredients and cover with lid. Cook on Meat/Stew setting for 90 minutes. Release the pressure on quick-release, and transfer meat to cutting board and shred with 2 forks. Divide the pork onto serving plates, add some sauce on top, and serve with steamed green beans on the side.

Nutritional Information per serving:
Calories: 243   Fat: 18g   Fiber: 1g   Carbs: 15g   Protein: 29g

Pork with Hominy

Cooking Time: 30 minutes
Servings: 6
Ingredients:
- 1 ¼ lbs. pork shoulder, boneless, cut into medium pieces
- 2 tablespoons chili powder
- 2 tablespoons almond oil
- Salt and pepper to taste
- 1 white onion, peeled, chopped
- 4 garlic cloves, peeled, minced
- 30 ounces canned hominy, drained
- 4 cups beef stock
- Avocado slices, for serving
- Lime wedges, for serving
- 2 tablespoons cornstarch
- ¼ cup water

Directions:
Set your instant pot on the sauté mode, add one tablespoon of almond oil and heat it. Add the pork, salt, pepper, and brown the meat on all sides. Transfer the meat to a bowl. Add the rest of the almond oil to the instant pot and heat it up. Add the garlic, chili powder, onion, stir and sauté for 4 minutes. Add half of the beef stock, stir and cook for 1 minute. Add the rest of the stock and return the pork to the instant pot. Stir and cover, and cook on Manual setting for 30 minutes.
Release the pressure naturally for 10 minutes. Transfer the pork to a cutting board, shred it using 2 forks. Add the cornstarch into instant pot, mixed with water. Set instant pot on sauté mode. Add the hominy, more salt, and pepper, and the shredded pork, stir and cook for 2 minutes. Divide among serving bowls. Serve with avocado slices and lime wedges.

Nutritional Information per serving:
Calories: 250   Fat: 8.7g   Fiber: 7.7g   Carbs: 29g   Protein: 32g

Pork Tostadas

Cook Time: 30 minutes
Servings: 4
Ingredients:
- 4 lbs. pork shoulder, boneless, cubed
- 2 cups diet cola
- ½ cup picante sauce
- 2 teaspoons chili powder
- 2 tablespoons tomato paste
- ¼ teaspoon cumin
- 1 cup enchilada sauce
- Corn tortillas, for serving
- Mexican cheese, shredded, for serving
- Shredded lettuce, for serving
- Guacamole, for serving

Directions:
In your instant pot mix 1 cup of diet cola with picante sauce, salsa, tomato paste, chili powder, cumin and stir. Add the pork, stir and cover. Cook on Meat/Stew setting for 25 minutes. Release pressure naturally. Uncover the instant pot, drain juice from instant pot, transfer the meat to a cutting board. Shred the meat with 2 forks. Return the meat to instant pot. Add in remaining diet cola and enchilada sauce, stir. Set the instant pot to sauté mode and heat well. Serve with tortillas, lettuce, cheese and guacamole.

Pork Tamales

Cook Time: 1 hour and 35 minutes **Servings:** 24 pieces

Ingredients:
- 8-ounces dried corn husks, soaked for 1 day and drained
- 4 cups water
- 3lbs. pork shoulder, boneless, cubed
- 1 yellow onion, peeled, chopped
- 3 tablespoons chili powder
- 2 garlic cloves, peeled, crushed
- 1 teaspoon baking soda
- ¼ cup shortening
- ¼ cup almond oil
- 4 cups masa
- 1 teaspoon cumin
- Salt and pepper to taste

Directions:
In your instant pot, mix 2 cups of water with onion, garlic, chili powder, salt, pepper, and cumin. Add in the pork and stir, cover the instant pot. Cook on the Meat/Stew setting for 75 minutes. Release the pressure naturally. Transfer the meat to a cutting board and shred it with 2 forks. Place pork in a bowl. Add one tablespoon of the cooking liquid from instant pot. Add more salt and pepper and set aside. In a bowl mix salt, pepper, masa, baking powder, shortening and almond oil. Combine using hand mixer. Add the cooking liquid from the instant pot and blend well. Add 2 cups water to instant pot.

Place the steamer basket inside of instant pot. Unfold 2 of the corn husks, place them on a work surface, add ¼ cup of the masa mixture near top of husk, press into a square and leave 2-inches at the bottom. Add 1 tablespoon pork in the center of the masa, wrap the husk around the dough and place it standing up in the steamer basket. Repeat with the rest of the husks, cover the instant pot and cook on the Steam setting for 20 minutes. Release the pressure naturally. Remove the tamales and place them on serving plates. Serve.

Nutritional Information per serving:
Calories: 150 Fat: 7.2g Fiber: 2g Carbs: 11g Protein: 7g

Pork Carnitas

Cook Time: 1 hour and 10 minutes **Servings:** 8

Ingredients:
- 3 lbs. pork shoulder, chopped
- 2 tablespoons ghee
- 1 jalapeno pepper, chopped
- 1 poblano pepper, seeded, chopped
- 1 green bell pepper
- 3 garlic cloves, minced
- 1 lb. tomatillos, cut into quarters
- 1 yellow onion, chopped
- 2 bay leaves
- 2 cups beef stock
- 1 red onion, chopped, for serving
- Cheddar cheese, shredded, for serving
- 1 teaspoon oregano, dried
- Salt and pepper to taste
- 1 teaspoon cumin
- Flour tortillas, for serving

Directions:

Set your instant pot on the sauté mode, add the ghee and heat it up. Add in the pork, salt and pepper. Brown the meat on all sides for about 3 minutes. Add the bell pepper, jalapeno pepper, poblano pepper, tomatillos, onion, oregano, garlic, cumin, bay leaves and stock. Stir and cover, cooking on the Meat/Stew setting for 55 minutes. Release the pressure naturally for 10 minutes. Transfer the meat to cutting board. Puree the mix from instant pot with immersion blender. Shred meat with 2 forks.

Add the meat back into the instant pot with the puree mix. Divide the pork mixture onto flour tortillas on serving plates. Add onion, cheese and serve.

Nutritional Information per serving:
Calories: 355   Fat: 23g   Fiber: 1g   Carbs: 10g   Protein: 23g

Instant Pot Balsamic Pork Tenderloin
Cook Time: 25 minutes   ***Servings: 4***
Ingredients:
- 2 lbs. pork tenderloin
- 2 tablespoons coconut oil
- 1 cup chicken stock
- ¼ cup balsamic vinegar
- 2 cloves of garlic, minced
- 1 tablespoon Worcestershire sauce
- ¼ cup water
- Sea salt and black pepper to taste
- 1 teaspoon sage, ground
- 1 tablespoon Dijon mustard

Directions:
Set your instant pot to the sauté mode, add the coconut oil and heat. Add the pork and brown the meat on all sides for five minutes. Add the remaining ingredients, and set to Manual setting for 20 minutes. When cooking is complete, release the pressure naturally in 10-minutes. Cut the pork into medallions and place on serving plates, cover with sauce from instant pot. Serve hot!

Nutritional Information per serving:
Calories: 347   Fat: 26g   Fiber: 1g   Carbs: 13g   Protein: 33g

Asian Pork Short Ribs
Cooking Time: 60 minutes   ***Servings: 4***
Ingredients:
- 4 lbs. pork short ribs
- 2 green onions, chopped
- 1 teaspoon coconut oil
- 3 garlic cloves, minced
- 3 ginger slices
- ½ cup water
- 2 teaspoons sesame oil
- 1/4 cup rice wine
- ½ cup soy sauce

Directions:
Set your instant pot onto saute mode, add coconut oil and heat it up. Add the green onions, ginger, garlic, and stir and cook for 1 minute. Add the ribs, water, wine, sesame oil and soy sauce. Stir and cook for 3 minutes. Cover the instant pot and cook on the Meat/Stew setting for 45 minutes. Release the pressure naturally for 15 minutes. Uncover the instant pot and

transfer the ribs to a plate. Strain the liquid from the instant pot, divide the ribs among serving plates and drizzle with sauce.
Nutritional Information per serving:
Calories: 300   Fat: 11g   Fiber: 1g   Carbs: 5g   Protein: 10g

---

Ribs & Coleslaw
Cooking Time: 35 minutes   **Servings: 4**
Ingredients:
- 2 ½ lbs. pork baby back ribs
- 1 teaspoon onion powder
- ½ teaspoon garlic powder
- ½ teaspoon chili powder

For the sauce:
- ½ teaspoon smoked paprika
- 1/3 cup apple cider vinegar
- ¼ cup coconut Aminos
- 2 garlic cloves, minced
- ¾ cup tomato paste

For the coleslaw:
- 2 green onions, chopped
- 2 carrots, grated
- Salt and pepper to taste
- 2 ½ teaspoons caraway seeds

- ½ teaspoon dry mustard
- ½ teaspoon paprika
- Salt and pepper to taste
- 2 tablespoons almond oil

- 6-ounces tomato paste
- 2 bacon slices, chopped
- 1 small yellow onion, chopped
- ½ cup water
- Salt and pepper to taste

- 3 cups green cabbage, shredded
- 1 cup red cabbage, shredded
- ¾ cup mayonnaise
- ¼ cup apple cider vinegar

Directions:
In a salad bowl, mix the green onions, carrots, with the cabbage. In a small bowl mix the caraway seeds with the mayonnaise, salt, pepper, ¼ cup vinegar and stir well. Pour over the coleslaw, and toss to coat, keep in fridge until ready to serve. In a bowl mix onion powder, paprika, dry mustard, garlic powder, chili powder, salt and pepper. Rub the ribs with this mixture. Set your instant pot to sauté mode, add in almond oil and heat it. Add the bacon and cook until done. Add in onion and garlic and cook for an additional five minutes. Place the ribs into your instant pot. Add some water, cover and cook on the Meat/Stew setting for 15 minutes. Add the remaining ingredients for ribs into instant pot and cook for another 10 minutes. Release the pressure naturally for 15 minutes. Transfer the ribs to a plate. Remove some of the sauce, leave enough in pot to cover bottom. Then place layer of ribs into instant pot and cover with layer of sauce until all the ribs are in the instant pot. Cover and cook on Manual setting for 10 minutes. Release pressure again, and divide the ribs among serving plates, and serve with coleslaw.
Nutritional Information per serving:
Calories: 360   Fat: 15g   Fiber: 1g   Carbs: 4g   Protein: 17g

Country-style Ribs
Cooking Time: 20 minutes
Servings: 8
Ingredients:
- 5 lbs. country-style ribs, boneless

For the brine:
- 1 tablespoon Truvia sweetener
- Salt to taste
- 4 cups water
- 3 garlic cloves, crushed
- 2 tablespoons liquid smoke

For the ribs:
- 2 tablespoons butter
- ½ tablespoon water
- 1 cup onion, chopped
- Cayenne pepper
- 1 teaspoon chili powder
- ½ teaspoon cinnamon, ground
- 2 apples, peeled, cored, sliced

For the sauce:
- 2 tablespoons yellow mustard
- 1 tablespoon liquid smoke
- 1 tablespoon Worcestershire sauce
- 1 teaspoon hot sauce
- 1 tablespoon Truvia
- 2 tablespoons Dijon mustard
- 2 tablespoons cornstarch
- 1 tablespoon soy sauce
- ¼ cup honey
- 2 tablespoons water

Directions:
In a bowl, mix the 4 cups water with some salt, and 1 tablespoon Truvia, garlic, and 2 tablespoons liquid smoke. Stir, and add the pork ribs and keep them in fridge to marinate for 2 hours. Set your instant pot to the sauté mode, add 2 tablespoons butter and melt it. Add the ribs and brown them on all sides. Transfer the ribs to a plate. Add the onions, ½ tablespoon water, stir, and cook for 2 minutes. Add the cinnamon, cayenne, chili powder, and apple slices. Return the ribs to the instant pot, cover and cook on the Meat/Stew setting for 15 minutes. Release pressure naturally. Transfer the ribs to a plate. Puree the onions and apples using a food processor, and set the instant pot on sauté mode again. Add the yellow mustard, 1 tablespoon liquid smoke, Dijon mustard, 1 tablespoon Truvia, Worcestershire sauce, hot sauce, soy sauce, honey and stir well. Add cornstarch mixed with 2 tablespoons of water, and cook for 2 minutes. Divide the ribs onto serving plates and drizzle with sauce. Serve.

Nutritional Information per serving:
Calories: 470   Fat: 34g   Fiber: 3g   Carbs: 10g   Protein: 29g

Pork Chops & Spinach Salad
Cook Time: 20 minutes **Servings: 6**
Ingredients:
For the pork chops:
- 6 pork chops, boneless
- 2 cups beef stock
- 3 garlic cloves, chopped
- 1 yellow onion, chopped
- 1 bunch mixed sage, rosemary, oregano, thyme
- 2 tablespoons ghee
- 1 teaspoon smoked paprika
- Salt and pepper to taste

For Spinach Salad:
- 1 large package of spinach leaves
- 1 English cucumber, sliced
- ½ red onion, thinly sliced
- Balsamic Vinegar dressing
- 2 large tomatoes, diced

Directions:
Set your instant pot to the sauté mode, and add in the ghee and heat it up. Add in the pork chops and brown them on all sides. Add the rest of the ingredients for porkchops into the instant pot. Set the instant pot to the Meat/Stew setting for 15 minutes. Meanwhile prepare the spinach salad in a large salad bowl adding all ingredients except for the dressing then keep in the fridge until ready to serve, just before serving add dressing and toss to mix. Release the pressure naturally. Put the pork chops onto a plate and remove and discard the herbs from instant pot. Place the pork chops back into pot and place on Manual mode, for 2 minutes. Stir. Divide the pork chops on serving plates along with spinach salad.

Nutritional Information per serving:
Calories: 410   Fat: 20g   Carbs: 29g   Protein: 30.2g

Pork Chops & Brown Rice
Cooking Time: 25 minutes **Servings: 6**
Ingredients:
- 2 lbs. pork chops
- 2 hot peppers, minced
- 1 tablespoon peppercorns, crushed
- 2 cups brown rice
- 3 garlic cloves, crushed
- 1 cup onion, chopped
- 2 ½ cups beef stock
- Salt and ground pepper to taste
- 3 tablespoons butter

Directions:
Set your instant pot to the sauté mode, add the butter and melt it. Add in garlic and onions, hot peppers and pork chops. Brown the meat on all sides. Remove the pork chops from instant pot once they are browned and place on a plate. Add the rice and beef stock to instant pot and stir. Add the porkchops back to the pot and set instant pot to the Meat/Stew setting for 25 minutes. Release the pressure naturally for 10 minutes. Add salt and pepper and divide porkchops and rice among serving plates. Serve.

Nutritional Information per serving:
Calories: 430   Fat: 12.3g   Fiber: 4.3g   Carbs: 53g   Protein: 30g

Braised Pork
Cooking Time: 75 minutes **Servings:** 6
Ingredients:
- 4 lbs. pork butt, chopped
- 16-ounces red wine
- 16-ounces beef stock
- 4-ounces lemon juice
- 2 tablespoons extra virgin olive oil
- 1 tablespoon paprika
- ¼ cup garlic powder
- ¼ cup onion, chopped
- Salt and pepper to taste

Directions:
In your instant pot mix the pork with the stock, wine, lemon juice, garlic powder, onion, oil, paprika, salt and pepper. Stir and cover, setting to the Meat/Stew mode for 45 minutes. Release the pressure naturally for 15 minutes. Stir the pork, divide into serving bowls. Serve.

Nutritional Information per serving:
Calories: 452   Fat: 44g   Fiber: 1g   Carbs: 12g   Protein: 27g

Chinese Barbecue Pork
Cooking Time: 50 minutes **Servings:** 6
Ingredients:
- 2lbs. pork belly
- 2 tablespoons dry sherry
- 4 tablespoons soy sauce
- 1-quart beef stock
- 2 teaspoons sesame oil
- 2 teaspoons Truvia
- 1 teaspoon peanut oil

Directions:
Set your instant pot on the Manual mode, add the sherry, stock, soy sauce and stir and cook for 8 minutes. Add the pork, stir, cover and cook on the Meat/Stew setting for 30 minutes. Release the pressure naturally, transfer the pork to a cutting board, allow to cool and chop into smaller pieces. Add the sauce in instant pot into a bowl and set aside. Set your instant pot to sauté mode, add in the peanut oil and add the pork back into the instant pot. Cook for a few minutes browning all sides of the meat. In a bowl mix the sesame oil with the sauce that was put aside and mix well. Add this mix to the instant pot and stir. Set on Manual mode for 10 minutes. Divide the pork onto serving plates, drizzle with sauce. Serve.

Nutritional Information per serving:
Calories: 398   Fat: 22g   Fiber: 1g   Carbs: 15g   Protein: 43g

Pork Roast with Fennel
Cooking Time: 1 hour and 20 minutes **Servings:** 4
Ingredients:
- 2 lbs. pork meat, boneless
- 5-ounces white wine
- 1 yellow onion, chopped
- 2 garlic cloves, minced
- Salt and pepper to taste
- 2 tablespoons extra virgin olive oil

- 5-ounces beef stock
- 1 lb. fennel bulbs, sliced

Directions:
Set your instant pot to the sauté mode, add the oil and heat it up. Add the pork, salt and pepper, stir and brown meat on all sides. Add the wine, garlic and stock to the instant pot. Cook for another few minutes. Transfer the pork to a plate. Stir the sauce in instant pot well. Return pork to pot, cover and cook on Manual setting for 40 minutes. Release the pressure naturally in 15 minutes. Add the onion, and fennel, to instant pot stir and cover. Cook on the Manual setting for 15 minutes. Release pressure again, stir and transfer the pork to serving plates. Serve with onion and fennel on the side with the cooking sauce from the instant pot drizzled over.

Nutritional Information per serving:
Calories: 426 Fat: 15g Fiber: 1.2g Carbs: 27g Protein: 36g

Pulled Pork
Cook Time: 1 hour and 20 minutes
Servings: 6
Ingredients:
- 3 lbs. pork shoulder, boneless, cut into chunks
- 8-ounces of water

For the sauce:
- 4-ounces hot water
- 2 teaspoons dry mustard
- Cayenne Pepper
- 1 tablespoon Truvia
- 2 teaspoons dry mustard
- 2 teaspoons smoked paprika
- Salt and pepper to taste
- 2 teaspoons Truvia
- 12-ounces apple cider vinegar

Directions:
Mix the Truvia with smoked paprika, 2 teaspoons dry mustard, and salt in a bowl. Rub the pork with this mixture and place the pork pieces into your instant pot. Add the 8-ounces of water and stir. Cover the instant pot and cook on the Meat/Stew setting for 75 minutes. Release the pressure naturally within 10 minutes. Transfer the pork to a cutting board and shred it using 2 forks. Discard half the cooking liquid from instant pot. In a bowl mix the 2 teaspoons of Truvia for sauce, with vinegar, cayenne, salt, pepper and hot water along with 2 teaspoons of dry mustard and stir well. Add to instant pot along with cooking sauce and cook on Manual for 3 minutes. Release the pressure naturally, and divide the pork among serving plates and drizzle with sauce from instant pot. Serve.

Nutritional Information per serving:
Calories: 428 Fat: 11g Fiber: 4g Carbs: 38g Protein: 31g

Creamy Pork Chops
Cooking Time: 20 minutes
Servings: 4
Ingredients:
- 4 pork chops, boneless
- 2 tablespoons extra virgin olive oil
- ½ small bunch of fresh parsley, chopped
- Salt and pepper to taste
- 1 cup sour cream
- 10-ounce can of cream of mushroom soup
- 2 teaspoons of chicken bouillon
- 1 cup water

Directions:
Set your instant pot to the sauté mode, add the oil and heat it up. Add in the pork chops, pepper and salt. Brown the meat on all sides. Transfer pork chops to a plate. Add the water and bouillon to the instant pot and stir well. Return the pork chops to the instant pot, cover and cook on Manual setting for 9 minutes. Release the pressure naturally, transfer the pork chops to a platter and set aside. Set the instant pot on Manual mode and heat up the cooking liquid. Add the mushroom soup, stir and cook for 2 minutes. Add the parsley and sour cream, stir and mix well. Pour over pork chops. Serve.

Nutritional Information per serving:
Calories: 282   Fat: 14g   Fiber: 1g   Carbs: 9g   Protein: 22g

Pork Chops and Onion
Cooking Time: 15 minutes
Servings: 4
Ingredients:
- 4 pork chops
- 1 lb. onions, sliced
- ½ cup milk
- 2 tablespoons extra virgin olive oil
- 1 garlic clove, minced
- 2 tablespoons parsley, fresh, chopped
- Salt and pepper to taste
- ½ cup white wine
- 1 tablespoon flour
- 2 tablespoons cornstarch mixed with 3 tablespoons water
- 2 tablespoons butter
- 2 tablespoons lime juice

Directions:
Set your instant pot on the sauté mode, add the oil and butter and heat up. Add the pork chops, salt and pepper. Brown the meat on all sides. Transfer meat to a plate. Add the onion, garlic to the instant pot and stir, cook for 2 minutes. Add the lime juice, wine, milk, parsley, and return the pork chops to the instant pot. Stir, cover and cook on Manual setting for 15 minutes. Release the pressure, add the cornstarch and flour, stir well. Cook on Manual mode for 3 minutes. Divide pork chops on serving plates drizzle with sauce. Serve.

Chapter 4. Lamb Instant Pot Recipes

Instant Pot Lamb Curry
Cook Time: 20 minutes **Servings: 6**
Ingredients:
- 1 ½ lbs. lamb stew meat, cubed
- 4 cloves of garlic, minced
- Cilantro, chopped
- 1 medium zucchini, diced
- 3 medium carrots, sliced
- 1 medium onion, diced
- ¾ teaspoon turmeric
- 1 ½ tablespoon garam masala
- 1 (14-ounce can) tomatoes, diced
- 1 tablespoon ghee
- Sea salt and pepper to taste
- Juice of ½ a lime
- ½ cup coconut milk
- 1-inch piece ginger, fresh, grated

Directions:
Combine your meat, grated ginger, minced garlic, lime juice, coconut milk, sea salt and pepper in a container with a lid. Mix ingredients and marinated in the fridge for 30 minutes. After marinating is complete, add the meat, tomatoes with their juice, marinade, ghee, garam masala, carrots and onions to your instant pot. Lock the lid in place, then set the steam release handle to 'Sealing' then select the Manual mode and cook at high pressure for 20 minutes. Once the cooking time is complete, allow your instant pot to release pressure naturally for 15 minutes, then flip the steam release handle to 'Venting' to release remaining steam before you attempt to open the lid. Remove the lid then set your instant pot to the sauté mode in the normal setting. Stir in the diced zucchini and simmer for 5-6 minutes without the lid or until the zucchini is tender and the sauce has thickened. Divide into serving dishes, over cauliflower rice, and garnish with chopped cilantro. Serve hot!

Nutritional Information per serving:
Calories: 230   Fat: 9g   Fiber: 3g   Carbs: 11g   Protein: 25g

Instant Pot Lamb Curry with Yogurt
Cooking Time: 25 minutes **Servings: 4**
Ingredients:
- 2 lbs. lamb, boneless, cubed
- 4 Chile pepper, chopped
- 2 tablespoons clarified butter
- 1 onion, diced
- 4 cups plain yogurt
- 1 teaspoon cumin seed
- 2 teaspoons ground turmeric
- 2 tablespoons coriander seeds

Directions:
Add the ginger, garlic, chiles, spices and yogurt into a food processor and process until well blended. Spoon the mixture over lamb, tossing to coat, place in fridge for 3 hours to marinate. Set your instant pot on sauté mode, add butter and heat it up. Add in the onions and brown them. Once onion is browned add in the lamb and yogurt marinade and mix. Place lid on instant pot and set to Meat/Stew setting for 20 minutes. Release pressure naturally for 15 minutes. Divide between serving dishes. Serve.

Nutritional Information per serving:
Calories: 260   Fat: 23g   Fiber: 12g   Carbs: 7g   Protein: 22g

---

Instant Pot Mediterranean Lamb Roast
Cooking Time: 60 minutes   **Servings:** 6
Ingredients:
- 4 lbs. lamb shanks
- 2 tablespoons olive oil
- 2 cups beef broth
- 1 teaspoon thyme
- 3 large sweet potatoes, peeled, cubed
- 1 teaspoon ginger
- 3 cloves garlic, minced
- 1 teaspoon sage
- 1 teaspoon marjoram
- Sea salt and pepper to taste

Directions:
Set your instant pot to sauté mode, add the oil and heat it. Add the lamb and swirl it around to coat with oil. Sear one side of lamb then flip it over to sear the other side. Sprinkle lamb shanks with all the herbs, sea salt, pepper and add broth. Cover the instant pot and set to Meat/Stew setting for a cook time of 45 minutes. Once cooking is completed release the pressure naturally for 10 minutes. Add the diced sweet potatoes. Close instant pot and set an additional cook time of 10 minutes on Meat/Stew setting. Release pressure again naturally for 10 minutes. Divide into serving dishes. Serve hot!

Nutritional Information per serving:
Calories: 254   Fat: 20g   Fiber: 9g   Carbs: 7g   Protein: 23g

---

Instant Pot Middle Eastern Lamb Stew
Cooking Time: 1 hour and 9 minutes   **Servings:** 4
Ingredients:
- 1 ½ lbs. lamb stew meat, cubed
- 1 onion, diced
- 2 tablespoons ghee
- 6 garlic cloves, chopped
- ¼ cup raisins
- 1 (15-ounce can) chickpeas, rinsed and drained
- 2 tablespoons honey
- ¼ cup apple cider vinegar
- 2 tablespoons tomato paste
- 1 teaspoon each: coriander, cumin, cinnamon, cumin seeds, sea salt and pepper
- 2 cups chicken stock or broth
- Garnish with fresh cilantro or parsley

Directions:
Set your instant pot to the sauté mode, add the ghee and heat it up. Sauté your onions for about 4 minutes. Add the lamb, spices, garlic, salt and pepper, and sauté for an additional 5 minutes. Brown the meat on all sides. Add the stock, vinegar, tomato paste, honey, chickpeas, and raisins, stir. Cover your instant pot and set to the Meat/Stew setting for 1 hour. Release the pressure naturally for 15 minutes. Remove lid and stir. Serve with cauliflower rice or quinoa and garnish with cilantro or fresh parsley. Divide into serving bowls and serve hot!

Instant Pot Lamb Rogan Josh
Cooking Time: 15 minutes   *Servings: 4*
Ingredients:
For the lamb:
- 1 ½ lbs. leg of lamb, cubed into small pieces

For the sauce:
- 1 tablespoon coriander, fresh, chopped for garnish
- 2 tablespoons tomato puree
- 1 1/2 cups water
- 2 tomatoes, finely diced
- 1 teaspoon each: ground coriander, ground cumin, ground ginger
- ½ teaspoon chilli, ground
- 4 tablespoons Greek yogurt
- ½ teaspoon garam masala
- ½ teaspoon garam masala
- 2 cloves garlic, minced
- 1 ½ teaspoons fennel seeds
- 1 ½ teaspoons cumin seeds
- 1-inch cinnamon bark
- 3 green cardamom pods, cracked open
- 1 tablespoon olive oil

Directions:
Mix the lamb, garam masala and yogurt for the marinade in a container with lid. Chill in fridge for 24 hours. When ready to begin cooking set your instant pot to the sauté mode, add the oil and all the whole spices. Sizzle and cook until the aromas are released, then in garlic and powdered spices. Cook for about 5 minutes, add in water, tomatoes, and tomato puree, stir. Add in the marinated lamb and stir before cancelling the sauté mode. Place the lid on your instant pot and set on Manual mode for 10 minutes. When cooking is complete press the quick-release to release the pressure. Once the pressure has come down then remove the lid and gently stir the lamb. Add sea salt to taste. Divide into serving dishes and garnish with chopped fresh coriander. Serve over cauliflower rice.

Nutritional Information per serving:
Calories: 231   Fat: 12g   Fiber: 4g   Carbs: 21g   Protein: 23g

Instant Pot Leg of Lamb Stew with Dates & Cinnamon
Cook Time: 1 hour and 40 minutes   *Servings: 4*
Ingredients:
- 2 lbs. leg of lamb, boneless
- 1 teaspoon each: black pepper, sea salt, ground cumin powder, ground coriander powder, turmeric powder
- 1 tablespoon balsamic vinegar
- 3 bay leaves
- 1 chicken stock cube
- 1 cup water
- 1 cinnamon stick
- 8 garlic cloves, peeled, whole
- 7 dates, dried
- 4 slices ginger root, fresh
- 1 red onion, sliced
- 1 tablespoon coconut oil
- Cauliflower rice or couscous to serve with
- 1 tablespoon almond flour to thicken sauce

Directions:

Rub the leg of lamb with cumin, coriander seed powder, turmeric, sea salt and pepper. Set your instant pot to the sauté mode, add coconut oil and heat it. Add the lamb and sauté, browning all sides of the meat. Add the onions, ginger around the lamb. Remove the lamb and add remaining ingredients to pot. Stir and bring to a boil. Press the Keep Warm/Cancel setting and return the lamb to the instant pot. Place the lid on the instant pot and set the Manual setting for a cook time of 80 minutes. Once the cook time is complete, release the pressure naturally for 5 minutes, then use the quick-release to let off the rest of the steam.

Remove the lamb to a cutting board, set the instant pot to the sauté mode and allow broth to bubble for 10 minutes, stir it a few times. Cut the lamb meat into bite-size pieces. Add the lamb meat back to the instant pot. Stir the lamb mixture, and turn off the instant pot. If sauce needs to be thickened add in the almond flour. Divide into serving dishes over a bed of cauliflower rice or couscous. Garnish with chopped coriander and serve hot!

Nutritional Information per serving:
Calories: 229   Fat: 11g   Fiber: 3g   Carbs: 23g   Protein: 25g

---

Lavender Lamb Chops
Cook Time: 25 minutes   **Servings: 2**
Ingredients:
- 2 lamb chops, boneless
- 1 tablespoon lavender, chopped
- 2 tablespoons ghee, melted
- 2 tablespoons coconut oil
- 2 tablespoons rosemary, fresh, chopped
- 1 teaspoon garlic, powder
- Zest and juice from 1 lime
- Zest and juice from 1 orange
- 2 cups water
- Sea salt and black pepper to taste

Directions:
Cover the trivet with aluminum foil. Set your instant pot to sauté mode and heat the coconut oil. Sear lamb chops for 2 minutes per side. Remove and set aside. Press the Keep Warm/Cancel button to end sauté mode. In a bowl, add the lavender, ghee, rosemary, orange zest and juice, lime zest and juice and seasonings. Pour 2 cups of water into the instant pot. Place the trivet inside the instant pot. Set the lamb chops on top of it. Close and seal the lid. Select the Manual setting and cook at high-pressure for 15 minutes. When cooking is completed, release the pressure naturally for 15 minutes. Divide onto serving plates. Serve hot!

Nutritional Information per serving:
Calories: 250   Fat: 5g   Dietary Fiber: 1g   Carbohydrates: 5g   Protein: 8g

---

Leg of Lamb & Spinach Salad
Cook Time: 40 minutes   **Servings: 4**
Ingredients:
- 1 tablespoons of ghee
- 3 lbs. leg of lamb, boneless and butterflied
- 2 garlic cloves, minced
- 1 teaspoon cumin, ground
- ¼ teaspoon thyme, dried
- Salt and pepper to taste

- 2 cups vegetable stock

For the salad:
- 4-ounces of feta cheese, crumbled
- ½ cup pecans, toasted
- 1 cup mint, chopped
- 1 ½ tablespoons lemon juice
- 2 cups baby spinach
- ¼ cup olive oil

Directions:
Rub the lamb with salt, pepper, 1 tablespoon melted ghee, thyme, cumin and garlic. Add the stock to your instant pot, add leg of lamb, cover and cook on high for 40 minutes. Leave the leg of lamb on a plate, and slice and divide between serving plates.
In a salad bowl mix the spinach, mint, feta cheese, olive oil, lemon juice, pecans, salt, pepper, and toss then divide amongst serving plates next to the lamb slices. Serve right away.

Nutritional Information per serving:
Calories: 234   Fat: 20g   Fiber: 3g   Carbs: 5g   Protein: 12g

---

Lamb Shanks & Carrots
Cook Time: 35 minutes   **Servings:** 4

Ingredients:
- 4 lamb shanks
- 2 tablespoons ghee
- 1 yellow onion, chopped
- 3 carrots, sliced
- 1 teaspoon oregano, dried
- 2 tablespoons tomato paste
- 2 garlic cloves, minced
- 2 tablespoons coconut flour
- 4-ounces of beef stock
- 2 tablespoons water
- 1 tomato, chopped
- Sea salt and black pepper to taste

Directions:
In a bowl, mix flour, lamb shanks, salt, pepper, and toss to coat. Set your instant pot to the sauté mode, add the ghee and heat it up. Add the lamb and brown all sides of the meat, then transfer meat to a bowl. Add oregano, carrots, garlic, onion, into instant pot and stir and sauté for 5 minutes. Add the stock, water, tomato paste, tomato and return the lamb to the instant pot. Stir, cover, cook on high for 25 minutes. Divide evenly between serving plates. Serve.

Nutritional Information per serving:
Calories: 400   Fat: 14g   Fiber: 3g   Carbs: 7g   Protein: 30g

---

Lamb & Coconut Curry with Cauliflower Rice
Cook Time: 28 minutes   **Servings:** 6

Ingredients:
- 3 lbs. lamb, cubed into small pieces
- 2 tablespoons ghee
- 2 cloves garlic, finely chopped
- 1 onion, finely chopped
- 1 teaspoon chilli powder
- ½ teaspoon coriander, ground
- 1 teaspoon cumin, ground
- ½ teaspoon turmeric, ground
- 1 cup full-fat coconut milk
- 1 cup beef stock
- 1 (14-ounce can) tomatoes, chopped

- 1 head of cauliflower, cut into rough chunks
- 1 tablespoon butter

Directions:
On your instant pot select the sauté mode, add the ghee to instant pot and heat. Add the lamb to pot and brown on all sides for about 5 minutes. Add the onion and garlic along with spices to pot and coat the lamb with them by stirring it all together. Add the stock, tomatoes, coconut milk to instant pot.

Change the setting to the Meat/Stew setting and set the cook time for 20 minutes. When the cooking is done, release the pressure naturally for 10 minutes. Meanwhile, add the cauliflower to a food processor and blend until it has the consistency of rice. Tip the cauliflower into a microwave-proof bowl, top with butter, cover and place in the microwave. Cook the cauliflower in the microwave for 3 minutes on high. Stir through the melted butter, adding some sea salt and pepper to taste. Serve the lamb curry on a bed of cauliflower rice.

Nutritional Information per serving:
Calories: 327   Fat: 11g   Fiber: 2g   Carbs: 9g   Protein: 26g

---

Instant Pot Lamb Chops with Creamed Cauliflower
Cook Time: 31 minutes   **Servings: 6**
Ingredients:
- 3 lbs. lamb chops
- 3 teaspoons sea salt
- 1 shallot, peeled, halved
- 1 cup beef stock
- 1 tablespoon tomato paste
- 2 tablespoons ghee
- 1 tablespoon extra-virgin olive oil
- 1 rosemary sprig
- Picked red onions for topping

For the Creamed Cauliflower:
- 1 head of cauliflower, cut into florets
- 3 garlic cloves, crushed
- 1 celery stalk, quartered
- 2 cups chicken stock
- Water
- 1 tablespoon unsalted butter
- ¼ cup celery leaves, chopped
- ¾ tablespoon cream
- ½ cup milk
- ½ teaspoon sea salt

Directions:
On a platter evenly distribute the rosemary leaves and salt on both sides of the lamb chops. Set your instant pot to the sauté mode, add the olive oil and butter and heat. Add the lamb chops and brown the meat on all sides for 12 minutes do chops in batches of 3. Once all the lamb chops are browned, and remove chops. Add the shallot, and tomato paste into pot stirring often. Add the beef stock. Return the lamb chops back to the pot. Cover and cook on high-pressure for 2 minutes. Once cooked use quick-release on the pressure. Meanwhile place the cauliflower, chicken stock, garlic, and celery into a pan. Add enough water to cover. Bring to a boil over medium-high heat, cook for about 15 minutes. Drain the liquid. Add cauliflower to food processor along with butter, salt, milk and cream. Puree cauliflower until it is creamy and smooth, then stir in the celery leaves.

Place the lamb chops on top of the creamed cauliflower, top with pan sauce and pickled red onions. Serve hot!

Nutritional Information per serving:
Calories: 312 Fat: 8g Fiber: 3g Carbs: 8g Protein: 26g

Instant Pot Cooked Lamb Tagine
Cook Time: 25 minutes **Servings: 6**
Ingredients:
- 3 lbs. leg of lamb, diced
- 2 tablespoons ghee
- 3 teaspoons cumin, ground
- ½ teaspoon cinnamon, ground
- 2 medium onions, sliced
- 2 garlic cloves, peeled and chopped
- 1 (14-ounce can) tomatoes, chopped
- 3 tablespoons honey, organic
- 1 beef stock cube
- 1 medium sweet potato, diced
- 6 no-soak dried apricots
- 1 ½ cups water
- Garnish with parsley, fresh leaf
- Lemon zest for garnish
- 1 (15-ounce can) chickpeas, drained, rinsed

Directions:
Set your instant pot to the sauté mode, add the ghee and heat. Add the lamb, garlic, onions, and sauté, browning meat on all sides, add the spices and stir well for about 5 minutes. Add the chopped tomatoes, honey, chickpeas, sweet potato, apricots, and crumble stock cube on top. Give it a good stir and mix well. Add water. Lock the lid on the instant pot and select the Meat/Stew setting with a cook time of 15 minutes.
Release the pressure naturally, for 15 minutes. Divide into serving dishes and garnish with lemon zest and fresh parsley leaves. Serve warm.

Nutritional Information per serving:
Calories: 323 Fat: 8g Fiber: 2g Carbs: 9g Protein: 27g

Lamb, Butternut Squash & Chickpea Tagine
Cook Time: 30 minutes **Servings: 4**
Ingredients:
- 2 lbs. lamb shoulder, cut into small chunks
- 1 (14-ounce can) chickpeas, drained, rinsed
- 1 small butternut squash, peeled, diced into small chunks
- 1 (14-ounce can) tomatoes, chopped
- 1 tablespoon coconut oil
- ½ teaspoon cinnamon, ground
- ½ teaspoon ginger, ground
- 1 teaspoon coriander, ground
- 2 teaspoons cumin, ground
- ½ teaspoon sea salt
- 1 tablespoon runny honey, organic
- 3 cloves garlic, crushed
- 1 onion, diced
- 1 cup water

Directions:
Set your instant pot to the sauté mode, add the coconut oil and heat. Add the onions and garlic, and allow to soften for 3 minutes. Now add the lamb and brown meat on all sides for another 5 minutes. Add spices and allow them to coat the meat, stir to blend.

Add tomatoes with 1 cup water and stir. Add in the honey and stir. Cancel the sauté setting. Put the lid on your instant pot and press the Manual setting with a cook time of 30 minutes. Serve with cauliflower rice or couscous with plain Greek yogurt on top and some fresh coriander, chopped. Divide into serving dishes. Serve warm.

Nutritional Information per serving:
Calories: 283   Fat: 10g   Fiber: 2g   Carbs: 10g   Protein: 24g

---

Lamb Tagine with Orange & Prunes
Cook Time: 30 minutes   ***Servings: 4***
Ingredients:
For Lamb Tagine:
- 2 lbs. lamb shoulder, cut into small pieces
- 2 teaspoons cinnamon
- 2 teaspoons turmeric
- 1 teaspoon ginger
- 2 medium onions, finely sliced
- 1 teaspoon sea salt
- ½ cup prunes
- 1 orange, peeled, and juiced
- 2 cups beef broth
- 2 garlic cloves, crushed
- 2 tablespoons ghee

For Cilantro Buttered Couscous:
- 1 large cauliflower
- ½ bunch cilantro, finely chopped
- 2 tablespoons butter
- 1 ½ teaspoons sea salt

Directions:
Add the spices to a large bowl and add the lamb meat. Mix and blend with hands to coat meat with spices then set aside. Set your instant pot to the sauté mode, add the ghee and heat. Add the garlic, and onions and sauté for 3 minutes. Add in the lamb mix to the instant pot and stir to blend ingredients. Brown the meat on all sides. Add the broth and stir. Cover the instant pot with the lid and set on Meat/Stew setting with a cook time of 30 minutes. When cooking is complete, release the pressure naturally for 15 minutes. Meanwhile cut the cauliflower into florets and place them into your food processor and pulse until the cauliflower has the consistency of large grain rice. In a pan heat the butter and add the cauliflower rice and cook for 5 minutes. Stir in the salt and add the cilantro just before serving. Serve the lamb over a bed of cilantro buttered rice. Serve warm.

Nutritional Information per serving:
Calories: 334   Fat: 15g   Fiber: 1g   Carbs: 11g   Protein: 29g

---

Lamb, Vegetable & Lentil Soup
Cook Time: 35 minutes   ***Servings: 8***
Ingredients:
- 2 lbs. lamb shanks, cut into small pieces
- 2 tablespoons coconut oil
- 2 cloves garlic, minced
- 2 carrots, chopped
- 2 celery ribs, chopped
- ½ cup peas, frozen
- 2/3 cup green lentil, rinsed, drained
- ½ cup dry white wine
- 5 cups water

- 5-ounces pancetta, chopped

Directions:
Set your instant pot to the sauté mode, add coconut oil, and heat. Add the lamb and brown the meat on all sides for about 5 minutes, then remove the meat from pot. Add the garlic, carrot, celery, pancetta, and onion into pot and sauté for about 3 minutes. Return the lamb to the pot along with wine and water, stir. Secure the lid on the pot and set on Manual setting with a cook time of 20 minutes on high pressure. When cooking is done use the quick-release to release the pressure. Add the lentils and set on Manual for a 10-minute cook time. Release pressure again using quick-release method and remove the lamb to cutting board, shred meat using 2 forks. Return the meat back to the pot along with peas. Cook for an additional 5 minutes on simmer setting. Season to taste. Pour into serving bowls. Serve hot!

Nutritional Information per serving:
Calories: 330 Fat: 25g Fiber: 24g Carbs: 5g Protein: 51g

Tuscan Lamb with White Beans
Cook Time: 25 minutes   **Servings:** 4
Ingredients:

- 2 lbs. lamb shanks
- 2 tablespoons ghee
- 1 medium onion, chopped
- 3 ½ cups water
- 1 cup navy beans, dried, picked over
- 2 rosemary sprigs
- 1 (14-ounce can) tomatoes, diced in juice
- 3 garlic cloves, thinly sliced
- 2 celery ribs, chopped
- 2 carrots, chopped
- Garnish with flat-leaf parsley, extra virgin olive oil for drizzling

Directions:
Set your instant pot to the sauté mode, add the ghee and heat it. Season the lamb shanks with salt and pepper and pat dry. Add the lamb to instant pot and brown the meat on all sides. Remove the meat to a plate. Add the carrots, celery, onion, and garlic to the instant pot and sauté for about five minutes, stirring often. Add the beans, water and salt and pepper to instant pot and stir. Return the lamb shanks to the instant pot and secure the lid of pot and set on Manual setting for 30 minutes. Release the pressure naturally for 10 minutes. Place the meat on a cutting board and shred the meat using 2 forks. Spoon the beans and vegetable mixture into serving bowls and top with lamb and sauce.

Nutritional Information per serving:
Calories: 317 Fat: 12g Fiber: 20g Carbs: 8g Protein: 38g

Moroccan Lamb Stew
Cook Time: 45 minutes   **Servings:** 4
Ingredients:

- 1 lb. grass-fed lamb, cubed stew meat
- 1 tablespoon coconut oil
- ½ lemon peel zested
- 1 bulb fennel cut into cubes
- ¼ cup raw almonds, toasted
- 3 tablespoons lemon juice,

- fresh squeezed
- ½ cup flat leaf parsley, fresh, chopped
- 20 green olives, pitted
- 2 turnips peeled, cubed
- ½ cup raisins
- 1 yellow onion, diced
- 4 carrots, peeled, sliced
- 14-ounces of pureed tomatoes
- 1 cinnamon stick
- ¼ teaspoon cloves, ground
- ¼ teaspoon cayenne
- 1 teaspoon black pepper
- Sea salt to taste
- 2 teaspoons cardamom, ground
- 1 teaspoon cumin, ground
- 2 teaspoons coriander ground
- 2 teaspoons smoked paprika
- 2 teaspoons ginger ground

Directions:
In a large container with lid, add lemon zest, coconut oil, ginger, paprika, coriander, cumin, pepper, cayenne, saffron, cinnamon stick, cardamom, and sea salt. Add the cubed lamb and mix well place lid on container and store in the fridge for 24 hours. When ready to begin cooking place the lamb mixture into your instant pot and layer the top of meat with raisins, turnips, carrots, fennel and onions. Mix the tomato puree with enough water to make 3 cups and slowly pour over meat mixture. Stir mixture. Set the lid on the instant pot and set it to the Meat/Stew setting on a cook time of 35 minutes. When the cooking is done release the pressure naturally for 15 minutes. Add the stew to serving bowls and top with chopped parsley, cilantro and toasted almonds. Serve warm.

Nutritional Information per serving:
Calories: 308   Fat: 9g   Fiber: 3g   Carbs: 9g   Protein: 29g

---

Instant Pot Rack of Lamb
Cook Time: 30 minutes   **Servings: 6**
Ingredients:
- 2 racks of lamb, about 1 lb, with about 8 ribs each
- ¼ teaspoon parsley flakes
- ¼ teaspoon black pepper
- ½ teaspoon seasoned salt
- ¼ teaspoon rosemary, ground
- ¼ teaspoon, marjoram
- ¼ teaspoon, savory
- ¼ teaspoon thyme
- ¼ cup water
- 1 tablespoon extra virgin olive oil

Directions:
Add the water to your instant pot, set racks into pot. Brush the lamb with olive oil. Mix the remaining ingredients in a small bowl. Coat the lamb with this mixture. Secure instant pot lid and set to Manual setting with a cook time of 30 minutes. When cook time is complete, release the pressure naturally for 10 minutes. Place racks on serving dishes. Serve.

Garlic Rosemary Lamb
Cook Time: 25 minutes **Servings:** 6
Ingredients:
- 1 rack of lamb
- ½ cup vegetable stock
- 4 carrots, chopped
- 4 garlic cloves, minced
- Salt and pepper to taste
- 2 tablespoons coconut oil
- 3 tablespoons coconut flour
- 4 pieces of fresh rosemary

Directions:
Season the lamb with salt and pepper. Set your instant pot to the sauté mode. Cook the lamb in instant pot along with garlic until brown on all sides for about 5 minutes. Add flour and stir. Add stock, rosemary, and carrots. Stir well. Close the lid and cook on Manual setting for 20 minutes. Once cooking is done, release the pressure naturally for 10 minutes. Remove the rosemary. Divide onto serving plates. Serve.

Nutritional Information per serving:
Calories: 287   Fat: 16g   Fiber: 9g   Carbs: 8g   Protein: 34g

---

Lamb Shanks with Garlic & Port Wine
Cook Time: 45 minutes **Servings:** 2
Ingredients:
- 2 lbs. lamb shanks
- 1 tablespoon ghee
- 8 garlic cloves, peeled and left whole
- ½ cup chicken stock
- ½ cup port wine
- 1 teaspoon balsamic vinegar
- 1 tablespoon rosemary, dried
- 1 tablespoon tomato paste
- Salt and pepper to taste
- 1 tablespoon unsalted butter

Directions:
Season the lamb shanks with salt and pepper. Set the instant pot to the sauté mode, add the ghee and heat. Add the lamb shanks and brown them on all sides. Add the garlic cloves. Add the port wine, tomato paste, stock, rosemary, and stir. Close the instant pot and set on Manual setting for 30 minutes. When cooking is done release the pressure naturally for 10 minutes. Remove the lamb shanks. Set the instant pot on cook for an additional 5 minutes to thicken the sauce, add in the butter and vinegar, stir. Serve the sauce over the lamb. Serve hot!

Nutritional Information per serving:
Calories: 282   Fat: 13g   Fiber: 10g   Carbs: 9g   Protein: 36g

Chapter 5. Poultry Instant Pot Recipes

Garlic Chicken
Cook Time: 35 minutes ***Servings: 8***
Ingredients:
- 2 lbs. chicken thighs, skinless, boneless
- 1 cup Parmesan cheese, grated
- 8-ounces cream cheese
- 1 cup chicken broth
- 1 teaspoon black pepper, freshly ground
- 2 teaspoons sea salt
- 2 teaspoons paprika
- 8 garlic cloves, minced
- 1 onion, diced
- 12-ounces cremini mushrooms or button mushrooms, halved
- ½ cup unsalted butter, melted
- Parsley, fresh for garnish

Directions:
Place your chicken thighs into your instant pot, and pour the melted butter over the chicken. Add the onion, garlic, mushrooms, salt and pepper, toss to coat the chicken thighs with butter. Cover and set on the Meat/Stew setting for 35 minutes.
Once the cooking is completed, release the pressure naturally for 15 minutes. Remove the chicken and vegetables to a serving platter. Set your instant pot to the sauté mode for 5 minutes. Combine the chicken broth, with Parmesan cheese and cream cheese. Cook, stirring, mixture until the cream cheese is fully melted. Pour the sauce over your chicken thighs and garnish with fresh parsley. Serve hot!

Nutritional Information per serving:
Calories: 495   Fat: 41g   Carbs: 6g   Protein: 26g

Ground Turkey & Basil Meatballs
Cook Time: 40 minutes ***Servings: 8***
Ingredients:
For the Sauce:
- 1 teaspoon parsley, dried
- 2 teaspoons basil, dried
- 2 garlic cloves, minced
- 1 tablespoon extra-virgin olive oil
- 1 (14-ounce can) tomatoes, crushed
- ½ stick of unsalted butter
- 1 cup heavy whipping cream
- Sea salt and black pepper to taste

For the Meatballs:
- 2 large eggs
- 2 cups cauliflower rice
- ½ teaspoon garlic powder
- ½ teaspoon black pepper, freshly ground
- 1 teaspoon sea salt
- 1 tablespoon Italian seasoning
- 2 cups Parmesan cheese, grated, divided
- ½ cup almond meal
- 12-ounces ground turkey
- 1 lb. Italian sausage, casings removed
- 8-ounces fontina cheese, cut into 24 cubes
- 2 tablespoons coconut oil

Directions:

In a mixing bowl, beat the eggs, then whisk in the almond meal, cauliflower rice, Italian seasoning, 1 cup Parmesan cheese, salt, pepper, and garlic powder. Add the sausage and turkey and mix to combine. Form 24 (1-inch) balls. In the center of each meatball stuff a fontina cheese cube, making sure the cheese is fully encased. Place the stuffed meatballs into your instant pot. Set your instant pot to the sauté mode, and add the coconut oil and heat it. Add the meatballs to the melted coconut oil, and brown them on all sides for 5 minutes. Add in the remaining ingredients to instant pot, except the heavy whipping cream, stir and place the lid securely onto instant pot. Set the instant pot to the Meat/Stew setting for a cook time of 30 minutes. When cooking is completed, release the pressure naturally for 15 minutes. Remove the meatballs from instant pot, and add the cream into the sauce in the instant pot and stir to blend. Add the meatballs back into the pot and set to the Keep Warm/Cancel setting until ready to serve. Serve hot!

Nutritional Information per serving:
Calories: 633   Fat: 50g   Carbs: 9g   Protein: 39g

Creamy Mushroom, Rosemary Chicken
Cook Time: 45 minutes   ***Servings: 6***
Ingredients:
- 2 lbs. chicken breasts, skinless, boneless
- 8-ounces bacon, diced
- 8-ounces button mushrooms, halved
- 1 cup sour cream
- Sea salt and black pepper to taste
- 3 fresh rosemary sprigs
- 6 garlic cloves, minced
- ½ cup dry white wine
- ½ stick butter, cubed
- 2 tablespoons coconut oil
- Fresh parsley, chopped for garnish

Directions:
Set your instant pot to the sauté mode, add the coconut oil and heat. Add the diced bacon to instant pot and cook until semi-crispy. Add the chicken and brown the meat for about five minutes. Add in the wine to instant pot and stir mixture. Add in the remaining ingredients, except for parsley, stir and secure the lid of instant pot. Set to the Meat/Stew setting for 35 minutes. When the cooking is complete, release pressure naturally for 10-minutes. Remove the rosemary sprigs and discard. Divide among serving dishes. Garnish with fresh chopped parsley. Serve hot!

Nutritional Information per serving:
Calories: 570   Fat: 49g   Carbs: 5g   Protein: 27g

Heavy Cream Chicken Stew
Cook Time: 40 minutes   ***Servings: 4***
Ingredients:
- 12-ounces whole chicken thighs and legs
- ¼ cup extra-virgin olive oil
- 1 teaspoon fennel seeds, crushed
- 1 tablespoon tomato paste
- 2 tablespoons dry white wine
- 2 garlic cloves, minced
- ½ onion, diced
- 1 stalk celery, chopped

- 1 cup black olives, pitted
- 1 cup chicken broth
- 1 cup heavy whipping cream
- 2 tablespoons fresh chopped parsley for garnish
- Sea salt and black pepper to taste

Directions:
Place the chicken broth, olives, celery, garlic, onion, white wine, tomato paste, fennel seeds, sea salt, black pepper, stir, then add in chicken pieces, and stir. Cover instant pot and set to Meat/Stew setting for 45 minutes. When the cooking is completed, release the pressure naturally for 15-minutes. Add in the heavy cream and stir. Divide into serving bowls, and garnish with fresh chopped parsley. Serve hot.

Nutritional Information per serving:
Calories: 447   Fat: 34g   Carbs: 7g   Protein: 26g

Ginger Spinach Chicken
Cook Time: 50 minutes   **Servings: 8**
Ingredients:
- 1 tablespoon ginger, minced
- 8 chicken thighs
- 2 cups baby spinach
- 1 teaspoon blackstrap molasses
- 1 tablespoon garlic powder
- 2 cups chicken stock
- Sea salt and black pepper to taste
- Chopped coriander, fresh, for garnish

Directions:
Add the chicken stock, salt, pepper, ginger, garlic powder, and mix, then add in the chicken thighs. Set the instant pot to Meat/Stew setting for a cook time of 45 minutes. When cook time is completed, release pressure within 10-minutes naturally. Add the spinach to the instant pot and stir, set on Manual for 5-minute cook time. Divide into serving dishes, and garnish with fresh, chopped coriander. Serve hot!

Nutritional Information per serving:
Calories: 472   Fat: 35g   Carbs: 3.8g   Protein: 32.7g

Ginger Coconut Chicken Wings
Cook Time: 50 minutes   **Servings: 6**
Ingredients:
- 3 lbs. chicken wings
- 8-ounces curry paste
- 2-ounces Thai basil, minced
- 1 tablespoon coconut milk
- 1 tablespoon ginger, fresh, minced
- 1 tablespoon cilantro, fresh, minced

Directions:
Add your chicken wings into your instant pot. In a mixing bowl, whisk together cilantro, coconut milk, ginger, curry paste and basil. Pour the milk mixture over your chicken wings and toss to coat. Cover and cook on Meat/Stew setting for 50 minutes. When the cook time is complete, release the pressure naturally within 15-minutes. Remove lid and stir. Divide into serving dishes, and serve hot!

Nutritional Information per serving:
Calories: 332   Fat: 14.3g   Carbs: 6.3g   Protein: 39.6g

Spicy, Creamy, Coconut Chicken
Cook Time: 40 minutes   **Servings:** 5
Ingredients:
- 1 lb. chicken thighs, boneless, skinless
- 2 tablespoons olive oil
- 2 teaspoons onion powder
- 3 garlic cloves, minced
- 1 tablespoon ginger, grated
- 3 tablespoons tomato paste
- 5 teaspoons garam masala
- 2 teaspoons paprika
- 10-ounces tomatoes, diced
- 1 cup heavy cream
- 1 cup coconut milk

Directions:
Cut the chicken up into pieces, and add to your instant pot. Add the grated ginger on top of the chicken pieces, then add the rest of the spices. Add the tomato paste, and tomatoes, along with olive oil, and mix well. Add half a cup of coconut milk and stir well. Secure the lid and set the instant pot on the Meat/Stew setting for 35 minutes. When the cook time is complete, release the pressure naturally for 10-minutes. Add to instant pot the heavy cream, and remaining coconut milk, stir. Replace the lid and set on Manual for 5-minutes of cook time. Divide into serving dishes. Serve hot!

Nutritional Information per serving:
Calories: 444   Fat: 33g   Carbs: 10g   Protein: 29.2g

Jalapeno, Curry, Garlic Chicken Meatballs
Cook Time: 45 minutes   **Servings:** 3
Ingredients:
- 1 lb. lean ground chicken
- 2 cloves garlic, minced, divided
- 1 tablespoon ginger, fresh, minced, divided
- 2 green onions, chopped
- 1 tablespoon cilantro, fresh, chopped
- ½ cup chicken broth
- 1 tablespoon basil, fresh, chopped
- 2 tablespoons almond meal
- 1 jalapeno, sliced
- 1 cup light coconut milk
- 2 tablespoons Thai green curry paste, divided
- Sea salt and black pepper to taste
- 2 tablespoons coconut oil

Directions:
Add to a mixing bowl, the ground chicken, green onion, cilantro, basil, almond meal, half the ginger, garlic, Thai curry paste, salt and pepper, and mix well. Divide the mixture into 12 equal portions and shape into balls. Add the rest of the ingredients into your instant pot, and mix well. Set your instant pot onto the sauté mode, add the coconut oil and heat. Add the balls into the instant pot.

Brown the meatballs for about 5-minutes, then remove the meatballs from instant pot. Add the rest of the ingredients into the instant pot and stir to combine. Add the meatballs, carefully back into the instant pot. Secure the lid and place on Meat/Stew setting on a cook time of 40 minutes. When the cook time is complete, release the pressure naturally for 15-minutes. Divide into serving dishes, and serve hot!

Nutritional Information per serving:
Calories: 284   Fat: 15g   Carbs: 3g   Protein: 33g

Chicken Breasts & Spicy Sauce
Cook Time: 25 minutes **Servings: 4**
Ingredients:
- 2 chicken breasts, skinless, boneless, chopped
- ¼ teaspoon ginger, grated
- 1 tablespoon garam masala
- 1 cup Greek yogurt, plain
- 1 tablespoon lemon juice
- Sea salt and black pepper to taste

For the Sauce:
- ¼ teaspoon cayenne
- ½ teaspoon turmeric
- ½ teaspoon paprika
- 15-ounce can of tomato sauce
- 4 garlic cloves, minced
- 4 teaspoons garam masala

Directions:
In a mixing bowl, add lemon juice, chicken, yogurt, 1 tablespoon garam masala, ginger, salt, pepper, and toss well, then leave in the fridge for an hour. Set your instant pot to the sauté mode, add the chicken, and stir and cook for 5-minutes. Add 4 teaspoons garam masala, paprika, turmeric, cayenne, tomato sauce, stir and cover. Set the instant pot to the Meat/Stew setting on a high cook time of 20 minutes. Once the cook time is complete, release the pressure naturally for 20 minutes. Divide between serving plates. Serve hot!

Nutritional Information per serving:
Calories: 452   Fat: 4g   Fiber: 7g   Carbs: 9g   Protein: 12g

Chicken & Spaghetti Squash
Cook Time: 20 minutes **Servings: 4**
Ingredients:
- 1 spaghetti squash, halved, seedless
- 1 lb. chicken, cooked, cubed
- 16-ounces Mozzarella cheese, shredded
- 1 cup water
- 1 cup keto marinara sauce

Directions:
Place a cup of water into your instant pot, add the trivet, add the squash, cover and cook on Manual setting on high for a 20-minute cook time. Shred squash and transfer it into a heatproof bowl. Add the marinara sauce, chicken, and mozzarella, toss. Add the squash back into the instant pot, along with marinara sauce, chicken, and mozzarella, stir and close the lid. Set to Manual setting for 5-minutes. Divide into serving bowls. Serve warm!

Nutritional Information per serving:
Calories: 329   Fat: 6g   Fiber: 6   Carbs: 9g   Protein: 10g

Chicken & Cauliflower Rice
Cook Time: 38 minutes **Servings: 6**
Ingredients:
- 3 lbs. chicken thighs, boneless, skinless
- 3 carrots, chopped

- 3 bacon slices, chopped
- 1 rhubarb stalk, chopped
- 4 garlic cloves, minced
- ¼ cup red wine vinegar
- 2 bay leaves
- 1 cup beef stock
- 1 teaspoon turmeric powder
- 24-ounces cauliflower rice
- 1 tablespoon Italian seasoning
- 1 tablespoon garlic powder
- ¼ cup olive oil
- Sea salt and black pepper to taste

Directions:
Set your instant pot on the sauté mode, add the oil and heat. Add bacon, onion, rhubarb, carrots, and garlic, cook for 8 minutes. Add the chicken and stir for 5 minutes. Add the vinegar, turmeric, Italian seasoning, bay leaves, and garlic powder, stir. Cover with lid and set to Meat/Stew setting and cook on high for 20-minutes. When cooking is complete, release the pressure naturally in 15-minutes. Add the cauliflower rice to instant pot with beef stock, stir, cover, and set on Manual setting and cook on low for 5-minutes. Divide into serving bowls. Serve warm!

Nutritional Information per serving:
Calories: 310   Fat: 6g   Fiber: 3g   Carbs: 6g   Protein: 10g

---

Chicken Curry
Cook Time: 30 minutes   **Servings: 4**
Ingredients:
- 2lbs. chicken thighs, skinless, boneless, and cubed
- 3 tomatoes, chopped
- 1 tablespoon water
- 3 red chilies, chopped
- 1 cup white onion, chopped
- 2 garlic cloves, minced
- 14-ounces canned, coconut milk
- 1 cup chicken stock
- 2 tablespoons coconut oil
- 1 tablespoon lime juice
- 1 teaspoon fennel seeds, ground
- 1 teaspoon cumin, ground
- 1 teaspoon turmeric, ground
- 1 teaspoon cinnamon, ground
- 2 teaspoons coriander, ground
- 1 tablespoon ginger, grated
- Sea salt and black pepper to taste

Directions:
In your food processor, mix the garlic, white onion, water, ginger, chilies, coriander, cinnamon, cumin, fennel, turmeric, black pepper, and blend until you have a paste and transfer it to a bowl.
Set your instant pot to the sauté mode, add the coconut oil, and heat. Add the mixed paste and stir and cook for 30 seconds. Add tomatoes, chicken, stock, stir and blend well. Cover and cook on Manual setting on high for 15-minutes. Add the coconut milk and stir mixture in pot. Cover the instant pot again and set on high for an additional 10-minutes more. Add in the lime juice, sea salt and black pepper and divide into serving bowls. Serve warm!

Nutritional Information per serving:
Calories: 430   Fat: 16g   Fiber: 4   Carbs: 7g   Protein: 38g

Chicken and Mushrooms
Cooking Time: 15 minutes
Servings: 4
Ingredients:
- 4 chicken thighs
- 2 cups button mushrooms, sliced
- 1 teaspoon Dijon mustard
- ½ cup water
- ½ teaspoon garlic powder
- Sea salt and black pepper to taste
- ¼ cup of ghee
- 1 tablespoon tarragon, chopped
- ½ teaspoon onion, powder

Directions:
Set your instant pot to the saute mode, add the ghee and heat it. Add the chicken thighs, onion powder, garlic powder, salt, pepper, and stir. Cook chicken on each side for 2 minutes, then transfer to a bowl. Add the mushrooms into your instant pot, stir and sauté them for 2 minutes. Return the chicken to your instant pot, add the mustard, water, and stir well, cover and cook on high for 10 minutes on Manual setting. When cooking is completed, release the pressure naturally, for 10-minutes. Add the tarragon and stir, divide between serving plates. Serve warm!

Nutritional Information per serving:
Calories: 263   Fat: 16g   Fiber: 4g   Carbs: 6g   Protein: 18g

Chicken and Salsa
Cook Time: 17 minutes
Servings: 6
Ingredients:
- 6 chicken breasts, skinless, boneless
- 2 tablespoons of olive oil
- 1 cup cheddar cheese, shredded
- Sea salt and black pepper to taste
- 2 cups jarred keto salsa

Directions:
Set your instant pot on sauté mode, add the oil and heat. Add the chicken, stir and cook for 2 minutes on each side. Add the salsa, stir, cover and cook on high on Manual setting. When cooking is completed, release the pressure naturally for 10 minutes. Spread the cheese over top of mix in the instant pot. Cook again for an additional 3 minutes more on high setting. Divide between serving plates. Serve warm!

Nutritional Information per serving:
Calories: 220   Fat: 7g   Fiber: 2g   Carbs: 6g   Protein: 12g

Chicken, Walnuts, and Pomegranate
Cook Time: 17 minutes   **Servings:** 6
Ingredients:
- 12 chicken thighs
- 3 tablespoons coconut oil
- 2 cups walnuts, toasted, chopped
- 1 yellow onion, chopped
- Juice of ½ a lemon
- ¼ teaspoon cardamom, ground
- ½ teaspoon cinnamon, ground
- 1 cup pomegranate molasses
- 2 tablespoons Truvia

Directions:
Place the walnuts in your food processor, blend and transfer to a bowl. Set your instant pot to the sauté mode, add the oil and heat it up. Add the chicken, salt and pepper and brown for 3-minutes on each side, transfer chicken to a bowl. Add the onion, walnuts, and sauté for 2-minutes. Add the pomegranate molasses, cardamom, lemon juice, chicken, Truvia and stir. Cover and set to Manual cooking on high for 12 minutes. When cooking is completed, release the pressure naturally for 15-minutes. Divide amongst serving plates. Serve hot!

Nutritional Information per serving:
Calories: 265   Fat: 6g   Fiber: 6g   Carbs: 6g   Protein: 16g

Turkey Instant Pot Stew
Cook Time: 33 minutes   **Servings:** 4
Ingredients:
- 2 tablespoons avocado oil
- 3 cups turkey meat, cooked, shredded
- Sea salt and black pepper to taste
- 2 carrots, chopped
- 3 celery stalks, chopped
- 1 teaspoon garlic, minced
- 1 yellow onion, chopped
- 1 tablespoon cranberry sauce
- 5 cups turkey stock
- 15-ounce can of tomatoes, chopped

Directions:
Set your instant pot to the sauté mode, add the oil and heat it up. Add the celery, carrots, and onions, stir and cook for 3-minutes. Add the cranberry sauce, stock, garlic, turkey meat, salt and pepper, stir, cover. Cook on Manual setting on low for 30-minutes. When cooking is completed, release the pressure for 15-minutes. Divide into serving bowls. Serve hot!

Nutritional Information per serving:
Calories: 200   Fat: 4g   Fiber: 1g   Carbs: 6g   Protein: 16g

Lemongrass Chicken
Cook Time: 20 minutes   **Servings:** 5
Ingredients:
- 1 bunch lemongrass, bottom removed and trimmed
- 1-inch piece ginger root, peeled and chopped

- 4-garlic cloves, peeled and crushed
- 1 tablespoon lime juice
- 1 yellow onion, chopped
- ¼ cup cilantro, diced
- 2 tablespoons coconut oil
- Sea salt and black pepper to taste
- 10-chicken drumsticks
- 2 tablespoons fish sauce

Directions:
In your food processor mix the lemongrass, with the garlic, ginger, fish sauce, five spice powder and pulse well. Add the coconut milk and pulse again. Set your instant pot to the sauté mode, add the coconut oil and heat it. Add the onion, stir and cook for 5-minutes. Add the chicken, salt and pepper, stir and cook for 3-minutes per side of chicken. Add the coconut milk, lemongrass mix, stir, cover. Set on the Poultry mode, and cook for 15-minutes. Release the pressure for 10-minutes naturally. Add lime juice, more salt and pepper and stir. Divide into serving plates. Serve warm!

Nutritional Information per serving:
Calories: 400   Fat: 18g   Fiber: 2g   Carbs: 6g   Protein: 20g

---

Chicken and Cabbage
Cook Time: 30 minutes   **Servings: 3**
Ingredients:
- 1 ½ lbs. chicken thighs, boneless
- 1 green cabbage, roughly chopped
- 1 yellow onion, chopped
- 2 chili peppers, chopped
- Sea salt and black pepper to taste
- 2 tablespoons ghee
- 1 tablespoon fish sauce
- 10-ounces coconut milk
- ½ cup white wine
- Cayenne pepper to taste
- 1 tablespoon curry
- 4 garlic cloves, peeled and chopped

Directions:
Set your instant pot to the sauté mode, add the ghee and heat it. Add the chicken, salt, pepper and brown on the sides of meat for about 5-minutes, then transfer chicken to a bowl. Add the chili peppers, onions, garlic to the instant pot and stir, cook for 3-minutes. Add the curry and cook for an additional 2-minutes, stirring. Add the coconut milk, wine, cabbage, fish sauce, salt, pepper, chicken, stir and cover, set to Poultry setting for 20 minutes. Release the pressure naturally, for 15-minutes. Stir and divide into serving plates. Serve hot!

Nutritional Information per serving:
Calories: 260   Fat: 5.5g   Fiber: 4.9g   Carbs: 15.2g   Protein: 30.2g

---

Chicken and Corn
Cook Time: 25 minutes   **Servings: 4**
Ingredients:
- 8-chicken drumsticks
- 2 tablespoons extra virgin olive oil
- ¼ cup cilantro, fresh, chopped
- 1 tomato, cored, chopped
- ½ yellow onion, peeled, chopped
- 3 scallions, chopped
- ½ teaspoon garlic powder
- ½ teaspoon cumin

- 2 corns on the cob, husked and cut into halves
- 1 tablespoon chicken bouillon
- 8-ounces tomato sauce
- 2 cups water
- 1 garlic clove, minced

Directions:
Set your instant pot on the sauté mode, add the oil and heat it up. Add the scallions, tomato, onions, garlic, stir and cook for 3-minutes. Add the cilantro, stir and cook for another 1-minute. Add the tomato sauce, water, bouillon, garlic powder, cumin, chicken, salt, pepper, top with corn. Cover the instant pot and cook on Poultry setting for 20-minutes. Release the pressure naturally for 15-minutes. Divide among serving plates. Serve warm!

Nutritional Information per serving:
Calories: 320   Fat: 10g   Fiber: 3g   Carbs: 18g   Protein: 42g

---

Duck Chili
Cook Time: 1 hour   **Servings:** 4
Ingredients:
- 1lb. northern beans, soaked and rinsed
- 5 cups water
- 2 cloves

For the Duck:
- 1 lb. duck, ground
- 1 tablespoon olive oil
- 1 yellow onion, minced
- ½ cup cilantro, fresh, chopped for garnish
- 1 bay leaf
- Sea salt and black pepper to taste
- 1 garlic head, top trimmed off
- 1 yellow onion, cut in half
- 15-ounces can of tomatoes, diced
- 1 teaspoon brown sugar
- 4-ounces canned green chilies
- Sea salt and black pepper to taste
- 2 carrots, chopped

Directions:
Set your instant pot to the sauté mode, add the oil, add carrots, chopped onion, season with salt and pepper and cook for 5-minutes, then transfer to a bowl. Add the duck and stir and cook for 5-minutes, transfer to a bowl. Put the beans into the instant pot, add the garlic head, onion halves, bay leaf, cloves, water, salt and stir, cover and cook on the Bean/Chili setting for 25-minutes. Release the pressure naturally for 10-minutes. Add back into the instant pot the duck, carrots, onions, tomatoes, chilies, stir. Cook on high on Manual setting for 5-minutes. Release the pressure again naturally for 10-minutes. Add into the instant pot the beans and brown sugar, stir. Add to serving bowls and garnish with fresh chopped cilantro. Serve warm!

Nutritional Information per serving:
Calories: 270   Fat: 13g   Fiber: 26g   Carbs: 15g   Protein: 25g

Chicken Gumbo
Cook Time: 45 minutes **Servings: 4**
Ingredients:
- 1 lb. smoked sausage, sliced
- 1 lb. chicken thighs, cut into halves
- 2 tablespoon olive oil, divided
- Sea salt and black pepper to taste

For the Roux:
- ½ cup almond flour
- ¼ olive oil
- 1 teaspoon Cajun spice

Aromatics:
- 1 bell pepper, seeded, chopped
- Tabasco sauce
- 1 yellow onion, chopped
- 1 celery stalk, chopped
- ½ lb. okra
- 15-ounce can of tomatoes, chopped
- 2 cups chicken stock
- 4 garlic cloves, minced
- 1 carrot, peeled, sliced

For Serving:
- ½ cup parsley, fresh, chopped
- Cauliflower rice, already cooked

Directions:
Set your instant pot on the sauté mode, add 1 tablespoon oil and heat it. Add the sausage, stir and brown meat for 4-minutes, then transfer sausage to a plate. Add the chicken pieces, stir, brown chicken for 6-minutes, then transfer to a bowl. Add the remaining tablespoon of oil to the instant pot and heat it up. Add the Cajun spice to instant pot, stir and cook for 5-minutes. Add the onion, bell pepper, carrot, celery, garlic, salt, pepper and stir and cook for an additional 5-minutes. Return the chicken and sausage to the instant pot and stir, adding in the stock and tomatoes. Cover the instant pot and cook on the Meat/Stew setting for 10-minutes. Release the pressure naturally for 10-minutes. Divide into serving bowls, on top of bed of cauliflower rice, and garnish with fresh chopped parsley. Serve warm!

Nutritional Information per serving:
Calories: 208   Fat: 15g   Fiber: 1g   Carbs: 8g   Protein: 10g

Chicken Delight
Cook Time: 37 minutes
Servings: 4
Ingredients:
- 6 chicken thighs
- 2 tablespoons coconut oil
- ½ teaspoon thyme, dried
- 1 cup baby carrots
- 1 celery stalk, chopped
- 1 yellow onion, chopped
- Sea salt and black pepper to taste
- 2 tablespoons tomato paste
- 1 ½ lbs. potatoes, chopped
- 2 cups chicken stock
- 15-ounce can of tomatoes, diced
- ½ cup white wine

Directions:

Set your instant pot to the sauté mode, add the oil and heat it up. Add the chicken pieces, salt and pepper to taste, brown the chicken for 4-minutes on each side, then transfer chicken to a bowl. Add the thyme, onion, celery, carrots, tomato paste to your instant pot and stir. Cook for 5-minutes. Add the wine, and cook for an additional 3-minutes, stir. Add the chicken stock, chopped tomatoes, chicken pieces and stir. Place the steamer basket in the instant pot, add the potatoes to it. Cover the instant pot and cook on the Poultry setting for 30-minutes. Release the pressure naturally for 15-minutes. Take the potatoes out of the instant pot. Shred the chicken, add it to bowl with potatoes. Divide among serving plates. Serve warm!

Nutritional Information per serving:
Calories: 237   Fat: 12g   Fiber: 0g   Carbs: 1g   Protein: 30g

---

Party Chicken Wings
Cooking Time: 25 minutes
Servings: 6
Ingredients:
- 12 chicken wings, cut into 24 pieces
- 1lb. celery, cut into thin matchsticks
- 1 tablespoon parsley, fresh, diced
- 1 cup yogurt
- ¼ cup tomato puree
- 1 cup water
- Sea salt and black pepper to taste
- 4 tablespoons hot sauce
- ¼ cup honey

Directions:
Add water to the instant pot. Place the chicken wings in the steamer basket of the instant pot, cover and cook on Poultry setting for 19-minutes. In a mixing bowl add honey, hot sauce, tomato puree, salt and stir well. Release the pressure naturally for 10-minutes on your instant pot. Add the chicken wings to the honey mix and toss to coat them. Add the chicken wings to a lined baking sheet and place under a preheated broiler for 5-minutes. Arrange the celery sticks on a serving platter and add the chicken wings next to it. In a bowl, mix the parsley, with yogurt, stir and place on serving platter. Serve warm!

Nutritional Information per serving:
Calories: 300   Fat: 3.1g   Fiber: 2g   Carbs: 14g   Protein: 33g

---

Roasted Chicken
Cook Time: 35 minutes
Servings: 8
Ingredients:
- 1 whole chicken
- 2 teaspoons garlic powder
- 1 tablespoon coriander
- 1 tablespoon cumin
- Sea salt and black pepper to taste
- ½ teaspoon cinnamon, ground
- 1 tablespoon thyme, fresh
- 1 cup chicken stock
- 1 ½ tablespoons lemon zest
- 2 tablespoons extra virgin olive oil, divided

Directions:
In a mixing bowl, add the cinnamon, cumin, garlic, salt, pepper, coriander, and lemon zest, stir well. Rub the chicken with 1 tablespoon of oil, then rub it inside and out with the spice mix. Set your instant pot to the sauté mode, add the rest of the oil to it and heat it up. Add the chicken to the instant pot and brown it on all sides for 5-minutes. Add the thyme and stock, stir, cover and cook on the Poultry setting for 25-minutes. Release the pressure naturally for 10-minutes. Transfer chicken to a platter. Pour cooking liquid over it from instant pot. Serve warm!

Nutritional Information per serving:
Calories: 260   Fat: 3.1g   Fiber: 1g   Carbs: 4g   Protein: 26.7g

---

Braised Turkey Wings
Cook Time: 20 minutes   **Servings:** 4

Ingredients:
- 4 turkey wings
- 2 tablespoons butter
- 2 tablespoons olive oil
- 1 ½ cups cranberries, fresh
- 1 cup orange juice
- 1 cup walnuts
- 1 yellow onion, sliced
- Sea salt and black pepper to taste
- 1 bunch of thyme, chopped

Directions:
Set your instant pot onto the sauté mode, add the oil and butter and heat up. Add the turkey wings, salt, pepper and brown them on all sides for about 5-minutes. Remove the wings from instant pot, add the walnuts, onions, cranberries, thyme to instant pot and stir and cook for 2-minutes. Add the orange juice and return the wings to the instant pot, stir and cover. Cook on the Poultry setting for 20 minutes. Release the pressure naturally for 10-minutes. Divide the wings among serving plates. Heat the cranberry mixture in instant pot with Manual setting on low for 5-minutes. Drizzle the sauce over wings. Serve warm!

Nutritional Information per serving:
Calories: 320   Fat: 15.3g   Fiber: 2.1g   Carbs: 16.4g   Protein: 29g

---

Braised Quail
Cook Time: 15 minutes   **Servings:** 2

Ingredients:
- 2 quails, cleaned
- 2 cups water
- 3.5 ounces smoked pancetta, chopped
- ½ fennel bulb, cut into matchsticks
- 1 bunch rosemary
- Sea salt and black pepper to taste
- 1 bay leaf
- 1 bunch thyme
- 2 shallots, peeled and chopped
- ½ cup champagne
- 4 carrots, cut into thin matchsticks
- Juice of 1 lemon
- Olive oil
- ½ cup arugula
- 2 tablespoons olive oil

Directions:

Place the carrot and fennel into the instant pot steamer basket. Add water to the instant pot, cover and cook on the Steam setting for 1-minute, release the pressure using quick-release, rinse vegetables with cold water and transfer to a bowl. Put the cooking liquid in a separate bowl. Chop half the rosemary and thyme, then set aside. Set your instant pot to the sauté mode, add the oil and heat. Add the pancetta, shallots, thyme, rosemary, bay leaf, salt, pepper, and cook for 4-minutes.

Stuff the quail with the remaining whole rosemary and thyme and add to the instant pot. Brown all sides of the quail for 5-minutes. Add the champagne, stir and cook for an additional 2-minutes. Add the cooking liquid from the vegetables, cover and cook on the Poultry setting for 9-minutes. Release the pressure naturally for 15-minutes. Remove the quail from your instant pot. Set the instant pot to sauté mode and cook the sauce for 5-minutes stirring often. Arrange the arugula on a platter, add the steamed fennel, and carrots, a drizzle of oil, lemon juice on top with quail. Drizzle the sauce from instant pot over the quail. Serve warm!

Nutritional Information per serving:
Calories: 300 Fat: 17g Fiber: 0.2g Carbs: 0.2g Protein: 40g

Crispy Chicken
Cook Time: 40 minutes
Servings: 4
Ingredients:

- 6 chicken thighs
- 4 garlic cloves, peeled, chopped
- 1 yellow onion, sliced thin
- 2 tablespoons cornstarch, mixed with 2 ½ tablespoons of water
- Sea salt and black pepper to taste
- 1 tablespoon soy sauce
- 1 cup cold water
- Dried rosemary
- 2 eggs, whisked
- 1 cup coconut flour
- 2 tablespoons butter
- 2 tablespoons coconut oil
- 1 ½ cups panko breadcrumbs

Directions:
In your instant pot mix the onion, garlic, rosemary and water. Place the chicken thighs into the steamer basket and place in the instant pot. Cover and cook on the Poultry setting for 9-minutes. Release the pressure naturally for 10-minutes. In a pan heat the oil and butter over medium-high heat. Add the breadcrumbs, stir and toast them, then remove them from the heat. Remove the chicken from instant pot; pat chicken thighs dry, season with salt and pepper, coat them with the flour, dip them in the whisked egg, then coat them in the toasted breadcrumbs.

Place chicken thighs on a lined baking sheet, bake in oven at 300° Fahrenheit for 10 minutes. Set your instant pot to the sauté mode, and heat up the cooking liquid. Add the salt, pepper, soy sauce, cornstarch and stir, then transfer to a bowl. Take the chicken thighs out of the oven, divide between serving plates. Serve with sauce from your instant pot. Serve warm!

Chicken Salad

Cook Time: 25 minutes
Servings: 2
Ingredients:
- 1 chicken breast, skinless and boneless
- 3 cups water
- 3 tablespoons extra virgin olive oil
- 1 tablespoon honey
- 1 tablespoon balsamic vinegar
- 3 garlic cloves, minced
- Sea salt and black pepper to taste
- 1 tablespoon mustard
- Mixed salad greens
- Half a cup of cherry tomatoes, cut into halves

Directions:
In a bowl, mix 2 cups water with a pinch of salt. Add the chicken to the mixture, stir and place in the fridge for an hour. Add the remaining water to your instant pot, place the chicken breast in the steamer basket of your instant pot, cover and cook on the Poultry setting for 5-m inutes. Release the pressure naturally for 10-minutes. Remove the chicken breast from instant pot. Cut the chicken breast into thin strips. In a bowl mix salt, pepper, mustard, honey, vinegar, olive oil, garlic and whisk well. In a salad bowl, mix chicken strips with salad greens and tomatoes. Drizzle the vinaigrette on top. Serve room temperature.

Nutritional Information per serving:
Calories: 140   Fat: 2.5g   Fiber: 4g   Carbs: 11g   Protein: 19g

Stuffed Chicken Breasts

Cook Time: 30 minutes
Servings: 2
Ingredients:
- 2 chicken breasts, skinless, boneless, and butterflied
- 2 cups water
- 1-piece ham, cut in half, cooked
- Sea salt and black pepper to taste
- 16 bacon strips
- 4 mozzarella cheese slices
- 6 pieces of asparagus, cooked

Directions:
In a mixing bowl, mix the chicken with 1 cup water, salt, stir, cover and keep in the fridge for an hour. Pat the chicken breasts dry and place them on a working surface. Add 2 slices of mozzarella, 3 asparagus pieces onto each, 1 piece of ham, add salt and pepper then roll up each chicken breast. Place the bacon strips on a working surface, add the chicken and wrap them in bacon strips. Put the rolls in the steamer basket of your instant pot, add 1 cup of water to your instant pot, cover and cook on the Poultry setting for 10-minutes. Release the pressure naturally for 10-minutes. Pat rolls with paper towel and lay them on a plate. Set your instant pot to the sauté mode, add the chicken rolls to the instant pot and brown them for 5-minutes. Divide among serving plates. Serve warm!

Nutritional Information per serving:
Calories: 270   Fat: 11g   Fiber: 1g   Carbs: 6g   Protein: 37g

Turkey Mix and Mashed Potatoes

Cooking Time: 50 minutes **Servings: 3**

Ingredients:
- 2 turkey quarters
- 1 cup chicken stock
- 1 celery stalk, chopped
- 3-garlic cloves, minced
- 1 carrot, chopped
- 1 yellow onion, chopped
- ½ cup white wine
- 2 tablespoons butter
- 3.5-ounces heavy cream
- 2 tablespoons Parmesan cheese, grated
- 5 Yukon gold potatoes, cut in halves
- 2 tablespoons cornstarch, mixed with 2 tablespoons water
- 1 teaspoon thyme, dried
- 1 teaspoon sage, dried
- 2 bay leaves
- 1 teaspoon rosemary, dried
- 2 tablespoons extra virgin olive oil
- Sea salt and black pepper to taste

Directions:
Season your turkey with salt and pepper. Add a tablespoon of oil to your instant pot. Set your instant pot to the sauté mode, and heat it up. Add the turkey and brown for 4-minutes, transfer turkey to a plate and set aside.

Add ½ a cup of chicken stock to your instant pot and stir. Add 1 tablespoon of oil, garlic, and cook for 2-minutes. Add the carrots, celery, pepper, salt and stir for 7-minutes. Add the sage, thyme, bay leaves and rosemary, stir. Add the wine and turkey back into the instant pot and the rest of the stock. Place the potatoes in the steamer basket for instant pot and place in the instant pot. Cook for 20 minutes on the Steam mode. Release the pressure naturally for 10-minutes. Transfer the potatoes to a bowl and mash them. Add some salt, butter, Parmesan cheese and cream, stir well. Divide the turkey quarters onto serving plates. Set your instant pot onto the sauté mode. Add the cornstarch mixture to pot, stir well, and cook for 3-minutes. Drizzle the sauce over the turkey and serve with mashed potatoes. Serve warm!

Nutritional Information per serving:
Calories: 200   Fat: 5g   Fiber: 4g   Carbs: 19g   Protein: 18g

Chapter 6. Seafood Instant Pot Recipes

Spicy Lemon Salmon
Cook Time: 10 minutes
Servings: 4
Ingredients:
- 4 salmon fillets
- 1 teaspoon cayenne pepper
- 1 tablespoon paprika
- 1 cup water
- Juice from 2 lemons
- Sea salt and black pepper to taste

Directions:
Rinse your salmon, and pat dry. In a mixing bowl, combine cayenne pepper, paprika, salt and pepper. Drizzle the lemon juice over the salmon fillets. Turn over fillets, repeat on the other side. Add 1 cup of water to your instant pot. Place the trivet inside your instant pot. Place your salmon fillets on top of the trivet. Close and seal instant pot, press the Manual button. Cook at high-pressure for 10-minutes. Once cooking time is complete use the quick-release for pressure. Divide up among serving plates. Serve warm!

Nutritional Information per serving:
Calories: 280   Fat: 20g   Fiber: 0.5g   Carbs: 8g   Protein: 20.5g

Coconut Shrimp Curry
Cook Time: 34 minutes
Servings: 4
Ingredients:
- 1 lb. of shrimp, peeled, deveined
- 10-ounces coconut milk
- 1 red bell pepper, sliced
- 4 tomatoes, chopped
- 1 teaspoon, fresh ground black pepper
- Juice from 1 lime
- 4 garlic cloves, minced
- 1 tablespoon coconut oil
- ½ cup cilantro, fresh, chopped for garnish

Directions:
Set your instant pot to the sauté mode, add the oil and heat it. Season your shrimp with lime juice, salt and pepper. Sauté the garlic for 1-minute. Add the shrimp and cook for 4-minutes per side. Add the bell peppers and tomatoes. Stir well. Press the Keep Warm/Cancel button to cancel the sauté mode. Add the coconut milk and stir. Close and seal the lid of instant pot. Press the Manual setting, and cook on high pressure for 25-minutes. Once cooking is completed, use the quick-release for pressure. Divide into serving plates, and garnish with fresh, chopped cilantro.

Nutritional Information per serving:
Calories: 150   Fat: 3g   Fiber: 3g   Carbs: 1g   Protein: 7g

Mediterranean Fish
Cook Time:
Servings: 4
Ingredients:
- 4 fish fillets (any kind)
- 1 teaspoon parsley, fresh, chopped
- 1 tablespoon thyme, fresh, chopped
- 1 tablespoon coconut oil
- 1 cup water
- 2 garlic cloves, minced
- 1 cup green olives, pitted
- 1 lb. cherry tomatoes, halved
- Sea salt and black pepper to taste

Directions:
Pour 1 cup of water in your instant pot. Cover the instant pot trivet with foil. On a flat surface, rub fish fillets with garlic. Season with thyme, pepper and salt. Place the olives and cherry tomatoes along the bottom of Instant pot. Place the fillets on the trivet. Close the lid and seal. Set on Manual, and cook at high-pressure for 15-minutes. When done, release pressure naturally for 10-minutes. Place the fish with ingredients, stir to coat them. Place on serving plates, and top with fresh, chopped parsley for garnish. Serve warm!

Nutritional Information per serving:
Calories: 225   Fat: 4g   Fiber: 2g   Carbs: 9g   Protein: 30g

Ginger, Sesame Glaze Salmon
Cook Time: 25 minutes
Servings: 4
Ingredients:
- 4 salmon fillets
- 2 tablespoons soy sauce
- 1 tablespoon rice vinegar
- 2 tablespoons white wine
- 1 tablespoon sugar-free ketchup
- 1 tablespoon fish sauce
- 4 garlic cloves, minced
- 2 teaspoons sesame oil
- 2 cups water

Directions:
In a mixing bowl, combine fish sauce, garlic, ginger, ketchup, white wine, rice vinegar, soy sauce, and sesame oil. In a large Ziploc bag, add the sauce and salmon fillets. Marinate for 10-hours. Pour 2 cups water in to your instant pot. Cover the trivet with foil. Place the trivet into your instant pot. Place the marinated salmon on the trivet. Close the lid and seal. Press the Manual button, cook on high-pressure for 15-minutes. Once done release the pressure naturally for 10-minutes. Divide onto serving plates. Serve warm!

Nutritional Information per serving:
Calories: 370   Fat: 23.5g   Fiber: 0g   Carbs: 2.6g   Protein: 33g

Cauliflower Risotto and Salmon

Cook Time: 30 minutes
Servings: 4
Ingredients:

- 4 salmon fillets, shredded
- 1 lb. asparagus, stemmed, chopped
- ½ cup parmesan cheese, shredded
- 1 cup chicken broth
- 1 tablespoon coconut oil
- Sea salt and black pepper to taste
- 2 teaspoons thyme, fresh, chopped
- 1 tablespoon rosemary, fresh, chopped
- 8-ounces coconut cream, unsweetened
- 1 head of cauliflower, chopped into florets

Directions:

In a food processor add the cauliflower florets, and pulse until you have rice-like consistency. Set your instant pot to the sauté mode, add the oil and heat it. Add the cauliflower rice, asparagus, and shredded salmon fillet. Cook until light brown and tender. Press the Keep Warm/Cancel setting to stop the sauté mode. Add the remaining ingredients and stir well. Close and seal lid. Press the manual button, cook on high-pressure for 20-minutes. Once done, release the pressure naturally for 10-minutes. Stir, and divide into serving bowls. Serve warm!

Nutritional Information per serving:
Calories: 225   Fat: 6g   Fiber: 4g   Carbs: 9g   Protein: 6g

Chili, Lime Cod

Cook Time: 22 minutes
Servings: 4
Ingredients:

- 4 cod fillets, shredded
- ¼ cup parsley, fresh, chopped
- ½ cup low-carb mayonnaise
- 1 tablespoon rice wine vinegar
- 1 yellow onion, chopped
- 1 celery stalk, chopped
- 4 garlic cloves, minced
- 1 can (14-ounce) tomatoes, diced
- 1 teaspoon paprika
- 1 tablespoon coconut oil
- 1 cup vegetable stock
- Zest from 1 lime
- Sea salt and black pepper to taste

Directions:

Press the sauté mode on your instant pot, and heat the coconut oil. Add the onion, and garlic. Sauté for 2-minutes, and add the celery and shredded cod. Press the Keep Warm/Cancel button to stop the sauté mode. Add the diced tomatoes, rice wine, mayonnaise, parsley, lime juice and zest, along with seasoning. Stir well. Close the lid and seal. Press the Manual button and cook at high-pressure for 20-minutes. Release the pressure naturally for 10-minutes. Divide onto serving plates. Serve warm!

Nutritional Information per serving:
Calories: 215   Fat: 5g   Fiber: 2g   Carbs: 3g   Protein: 35g

Instant Pot Halibut Fillets
Cook Time: 30 minutes
Servings: 4
Ingredients:
- 4 halibut fillets
- 1 lemon sliced for garnish
- 2 cups of water
- Zest and juice of 1 lime
- ¼ cup mozzarella cheese, grated
- ¼ cup parmesan cheese, fresh, grated
- ¼ cup ghee, melted
- ¼ cup low-carb mayonnaise
- 4 green onions, chopped
- 6 garlic cloves, minced
- Sea salt and black pepper to taste

Directions:
Pour 2-cups of water in the instant pot. Cover the trivet with foil. In mixing bowl, combine green onions, garlic, ghee, mayonnaise, cheeses, lime juice, lime zest, salt and pepper. Stir well. Coat the halibut fillets with the mixture. Place halibut on trivet. Close and seal the lid. Press the Manual button, cook on high-pressure for 20-minutes. Use the quick-release for pressure. Divide up into serving plates, and garnish with fresh, chopped parsley. Serve warm!

Nutritional Information per serving:
Calories: 250   Fat: 12g   Fiber: 1g   Carbs: 5g   Protein: 25g

Fish Fillets & Orange Sauce
Cook Time: 10 minutes
Servings: 4
Ingredients:
- 4 spring onions, finely chopped
- Zest from 1 orange
- Juice from 1 orange
- 4 white fish fillets
- 1 tablespoon olive oil
- 1-inch ginger piece, grated
- Sea salt and black pepper to taste
- 1 cup fish stock

Directions:
Season the fish fillets with salt and pepper, then rub them with oil and place on a plate. Place the onions, orange zest, orange juice, fish stock into your instant pot. Add the steamer basket and place the fish fillets inside it. Cover the instant pot with lid and cook on high-pressure on Manual setting for 10-minutes. Release the pressure using the quick-release. Divide the fish fillets among serving plates, then drizzle the orange sauce from instant pot over fillets. Serve warm!

Nutritional Information per serving:
Calories: 343   Fat: 21g   Fiber: 1g   Carbs: 8g   Protein: 26g

Calamari & Tomatoes
Cook Time: 30 minutes
Servings: 4
Ingredients:

- 1 ½ lbs. of calamari, cleaned, heads detached, tentacles separated and cut into thin strips
- 1 tablespoon olive oil
- Juice of 1 lemon
- 2 anchovies, chopped
- A pinch of red pepper flakes
- 1 bunch parsley, chopped
- ½ cup white wine
- 1 garlic clove, minced
- Sea salt and black pepper to taste
- 1 (15-ounce can) tomatoes, chopped

Directions:
Set your instant pot to the sauté mode, add the oil and heat it up. Add the anchovies, garlic, and pepper flakes, stir and cook for 3-minutes. Add the calamari, stir and sauté for 5-minutes more. Add the wine, stir and cook for 3 minutes more. Add the tomatoes, half of the parsley, some salt and pepper, stir and cover pot. Set to manual on high-pressure for 20-minutes. Release the pressure naturally for 15-minutes. Add the lemon juice and zest, remaining parsley and stir. Divide up among serving plates. Serve warm!

Nutritional Information per serving:
Calories: 342   Fat: 18g   Fiber: 1g   Carbs: 3g   Protein: 28g

Red Snapper & Chili Sauce
Cook Time: 12 minutes
Servings: 2
Ingredients:

- 1 red snapper, cleaned
- 1 teaspoon Truvia
- 2 cups water
- 1 green onion, chopped
- 1 teaspoon sesame oil
- 2 teaspoons sesame seeds, toasted
- 2 teaspoons Korean plum extract
- ½ teaspoon ginger, grated
- 1 garlic clove, minced
- 1 tablespoon soy sauce
- 3 tablespoons Korean chili paste
- Dash of sea salt

Directions:
Make some slits into your red snapper, season with salt and leave aside for 30-minutes. Put the water into your instant pot, add the steamer basket inside and place the fish in it. Rub the fish with the chili paste, cover your instant pot with lid and secure and cook on Manual on low for 12-minutes. In a mixing bowl, combine Truvia, soy sauce, garlic, plum extract, sesame seeds, sesame oil, green onions, and stir well. Release pressure naturally for 10-minutes. Divide fish among serving plates, and drizzle with sauce you made. Serve warm!

Baked Red Snapper
Cook Time: 12 minutes
Servings: 4
Ingredients:
- 4 red snappers, cleaned
- 5 garlic cloves, minced
- ½ cup parsley, chopped
- ½ cup olive oil
- 1 lemon, sliced
- 4 tablespoons lemon juice
- Sea salt and black pepper to taste
- 5-ounces of grape leaves, blanched

Directions:
Pat the fish dry and place it in a bowl. Season the fish with salt, pepper, and brush half the oil onto it and rub well, then keep in the fridge for 30-minutes. In a mixing bowl, combine parsley, salt and pepper, stir. Divide this mix into the fish cavities, wrap each in a grape leaf, drizzle with lemon juice over them and place the fish in a heat-proof dish within your instant pot steamer basket. Drizzle the rest of the oil over the fish, cover the dish with some tin foil, place the basket inside your instant pot. Add 2 cups of water to your instant pot, cover with lid, and cook on High-pressure for 12-minutes. Release the pressure using the quick-release. Divide the wrapped fish among serving plates, top with lemon slices. Serve warm!

Nutritional Information per serving:
Calories: 276   Fat: 20g   Fiber: 1g   Carbs: 8g   Protein: 29g

Red Snapper & Tomato Sauce
Cook Time: 11 minutes
Servings: 4
Ingredients:
- 4 medium red snapper fillets
- 4 ciabatta rolls, cut in halves, and toasted
- 2 tablespoons parsley, fresh, chopped
- 16-ounces canned tomatoes, crushed
- ¼ cup olive oil
- 1 yellow onion, chopped
- 3 tablespoons hot water
- A pinch of saffron threads
- Sea salt and black pepper to taste

Directions:
In a mixing bowl, combine, hot water, and saffron, then leave aside. Set your instant pot to the sauté mode, and add the oil and heat it up. Add the onion, and stir and cook for 2-minutes. Add the fish, cook for an additional 2-minutes and flip on the other side and cook that side for 2-minutes. Add the tomatoes, drained saffron, some salt and pepper, cover the instant pot with lid. Set the instant pot to low for 5-minutes. Release the pressure with the quick-release. Divide the fish and sauce among serving plates, and garnish with fresh, chopped parsley, serve with ciabatta rolls. Serve warm!

Thai Red Snapper
Cook Time: 20 minutes **Servings: 2**
Ingredients:
For the Marinade:
- 1 tablespoon Thai curry paste
- 1 cup coconut milk
- 1 tablespoon fish sauce paste
- 1 tablespoon cilantro, chopped
- 2 cups water
- 1 lime, sliced

For the Salsa:
- 2 jalapenos, chopped
- 2 mangoes, peeled, and chopped
- 1 scallion, chopped
- 2 red snapper fillets
- 1 teaspoon garlic, minced
- 1 tablespoon ginger, grated
- 1 teaspoon Truvia
- Juice of ½ a lime
- Zest of a lime
- A handful of cilantro, fresh, chopped for garnish
- Juice from 1 lime

Directions:
In a mixing bowl, combine fish sauce with coconut milk, zest from 1 lime, curry paste, juice from ½ a lime, Truvia, garlic, ginger, and whisk well. Add the fish fillets, toss to coat and set aside for 30-minutes. In another bowl, mix jalapenos, mangoes, scallion, juice from 1 lime, mix well and leave aside. Place the water in your instant pot and put the steamer basket inside. Place the fish in 2-pieces of parchment paper, cover them with lime slices and wrap them. Place them into the steamer basket, cover the instant pot with lid, and cook on high for 10-minutes. Release the pressure using the quick-release. Put the marinade from fish into a pan and heat it up over medium-high heat. Boil for a couple of minutes and take off heat. Drizzle some of the sauce over dish, top with mango salsa and garnish with fresh, chopped cilantro. Serve warm!

Nutritional Information per serving:
Calories: 257   Fat: 17g   Fiber: 1g   Carbs: 10g   Protein: 28g

---

Lobster & Sweet Potatoes
Cook Time: 16 minutes **Servings: 4**
Ingredients:
- 4 lobsters
- 1 onion, cut into wedges
- Water
- 2 garlic heads, not peeled
- 1 ½ lbs of sweet potatoes, peeled, and cubed
- 4 ears of corn, shucked, and halved
- 4 tablespoons butter

Directions:
Place the cubed-sweet potatoes in your instant pot. Add onion, garlic, and some salt with enough water to cover them. Cover your pot and cook on high for 12-minutes. Release the pressure using quick-release. Add the lobsters, and corn to the instant pot and cover once again. Cook on high for 5-minutes. Release the pressure again using quick-release. Divide the corn and sweet potatoes among serving plates, season with some salt and drizzle some

melted butter over them. Discard the onion, and garlic. Transfer the lobsters to cutting board and remove the meat. Divide lobster meat among serving plates next to corn and sweet potatoes. Drizzle the rest of butter over lobster meat. Serve warm!

Nutritional Information per serving:
Calories: 297   Fat: 18g   Fiber: 2g   Carbs: 11g   Protein: 32g

---

Steamed Lobster
Cooking Time: 3 minutes
Servings: 1
Ingredients:
- 1 cup non-alcoholic beer
- 2 cups water
- 1 lobster
- Sea salt and white pepper to taste

Directions:
Add the beer and water to your instant pot and place the steamer basket inside it as well. Place the lobster in the basket, cover and cook on high for 3-minutes. Release the pressure with quick-release. Transfer lobster to serving plate and season with some salt and pepper. Serve warm!

Nutritional Information per serving:
Calories: 286   Fat: 19g   Fiber: 1g   Carbs: 16g   Protein: 37g

---

Simple Instant Pot Lobster
Cook Time: 3 minutes
Servings: 3
Ingredients:
- 2 lbs. lobster tails
- ½ cup ghee, melted
- 1 cup water
- A dash of sea salt and some black pepper

Directions:
Put the water into your instant pot, add the lobster tails into steamer basket and place in your instant pot. Cook on high for 3-minutes. Release the pressure using the quick-release. Transfer the lobster tails to a bowl, drizzle melted ghee over lobster, and sprinkle with some salt and pepper. Serve warm!

Nutritional Information per serving:
Calories: 289   Fat: 14g   Fiber: 2g   Carbs: 8g   Protein: 30g

Spicy Sardines
Cook Time: 15 minutes
Servings: 4
Ingredients:
- 1 lb. of sardines
- 8 garlic cloves, minced
- 2 yellow onions, cut in halves, then thinly sliced
- 2 tablespoons white vinegar
- 3 tablespoons coconut oil
- ½ teaspoon turmeric
- 1 large tomato, chopped
- 1 ½ teaspoons chili powder
- 4 curry leaves
- 1 green chili pepper, chopped
- 1-inch ginger pieces, grated

Directions:
Place the oil into your instant pot, and heat it up on the sauté mode. Add the garlic, ginger, onion, curry leaves, chili, and stir for 2-minutes. Add the chili powder, tomato, turmeric, vinegar, salt, pepper, and stir and cook for an additional 3-minutes. Add the sardines, cover your instant pot and cook on high for 10-minutes. Release the pressure with quick-release. Divide among serving plates. Serve warm!

Nutritional Information per serving:
Calories: 206 Fat: 11g Fiber: 2g Carbs: 13g Protein: 27g

Tasty Sardines
Cook Time: 20 minutes
Servings: 5
Ingredients:
- 2 lbs. sardines
- 2 peppercorns
- 10 garlic cloves, minced
- 1 tablespoon, smoked paprika
- 1 teaspoon Truvia
- 1 red chili pepper, chopped
- 2 bay leaves
- 1 pickle, sliced
- 1 carrot, chopped
- 2 cups tomato sauce
- 2 tablespoons olive oil
- 2 cups water

Directions:
Put sardines into a mixing bowl, cover them with water and salt to taste, leave them to sit for 15-minutes. Drain the sardines and put them into your instant pot. Add the peppercorns, cloves, oil, tomato sauce, carrots, bay leaves, chili pepper, pickle, Truvia, paprika, garlic, and stir gently. Cover with pot lid and cook on low for 20-minutes. Release the pressure naturally for 10-minutes. Divide among serving plates. Serve warm!

Nutritional Information per serving:
Calories: 284 Fat: 12g Fiber: 1g Carbs: 14g Protein: 29g

Teriyaki Salmon
Cook Time: 10 minutes
Servings: 2
Ingredients:
- ¼ cup water
- 2 teaspoons sesame seeds
- 1 tablespoon sesame oil
- 1 garlic clove, minced
- ½ cup soy sauce
- 2 salmon fillets
- 1 tablespoon cornstarch mixed with 1 tablespoon of water
- 3 green onions, chopped
- 1 cup water for instant pot
- 1 teaspoon Truvia
- 1 tablespoon ginger, grated
- ¼ cup mirin

Directions:
In a mixing bowl, combine mirin, soy sauce, sesame oil, sesame seeds, ginger, garlic, Truvia, and ¼ cup water, stir well. Add the salmon and toss to coat, cover and keep the salmon in the fridge for 30-minutes. Add 1 cup water to your instant pot and place the steamer basket inside. Add a pan in the basket, put the salmon in the pan and reserve the marinade. Cover your instant pot with lid and cook on high for 8-minutes. Put the marinade in a pot and heat it over medium-high heat. Add the cornstarch to it, mix and stir. Release the pressure using quick-release. Divide the salmon among serving plates, and drizzle with the sauce on top. Serve warm!

Nutritional Information per serving:
Calories: 304   Fat: 21g   Fiber: 2g   Carbs: 16g   Protein: 46g

Simple Salmon & Onion
Cook Time: 6 minutes
Servings: 4
Ingredients:
- 4 salmon steaks
- ½ cup white wine
- 1 yellow onion, sliced thinly
- ½ cup water
- 1 lemon, sliced
- Sea salt and black pepper to taste

Directions:
Add the wine, water, and some salt and pepper into your instant pot. Stir, and place the steamer basket inside your instant pot. Put the salmon steaks in the basket, season with salt and pepper, cover them with onions, and lemon slices. Cover and cook on high for 6-minutes. Release the pressure using quick-release. Divide the salmon steaks among serving plates and top them with onions and lemon slices. Serve warm!

Nutritional Information per serving:
Calories: 321   Fat: 19g   Fiber: 1g   Carbs: 12g   Protein: 43g

Simple Instant Pot Salmon
Cook Time: 5 minutes
Servings: 2
Ingredients:
- 2 salmon fillets
- 1 tablespoon thyme, fresh, chopped
- 1 bay leaf
- 2 tablespoons mustard
- Sea salt and black pepper to taste
- 1 cup fish stock
- Slices of lemon for garnish

Directions:
In a mixing bowl, combine mustard, thyme, salt, pepper, and stir. Rub the salmon fillets with this mix. Put the stock and bay leaf into your instant pot. Place the steamer basket inside instant pot and place salmon in it. Cover and cook on high for 5 minutes. Release the pressure using quick-release. Divide the salmon among serving plates and garnish with sliced lemons. Serve warm!

Nutritional Information per serving:
Calories: 326   Fat: 20g   Fiber: 2g   Carbs: 14g   Protein: 47g

Chapter 7. Soup Instant Pot Recipes

Sweet Potato & Broccoli Soup
Cook Time: 40 minutes
Servings: 4
Ingredients:
- 2 lbs. sweet potatoes, peeled, cubed
- 1 cup cheddar cheese, grated, divided
- 4 cups veggie broth
- 2 tablespoons butter
- 1 broccoli head, chopped into florets
- 2 garlic cloves, minced
- 1 cup half and half

Directions:
Set the instant pot to the sauté mode, add the butter and heat it. Add the garlic and cook it for 2-minutes. Stir in the broth and broccoli, add the sweet potatoes. Close the lid and select Manual, cook on high for 5-minutes. To release the pressure, use the quick-release. Stir the half and half cream in a bowl with half of the cheese, and blend with blender. Add to the instant pot and stir. Divide among serving bowls, and garnish with remaining cheddar cheese. Serve warm!

Nutritional Information per serving:
Calories: 522   Fat: 35g   Carbs: 23g   Protein: 28g

Squash & Potato Soup
Cook Time: 40 minutes
Servings: 4
Ingredients:
- 2 cups of sweet potatoes
- 2 cups butternut squash
- 2 garlic cloves, minced
- 2 tablespoons coconut oil
- 3 cups bone broth
- ½ teaspoon turmeric
- ½ teaspoon nutmeg
- 1 teaspoon tarragon
- 1 ½ teaspoon curry powder
- 1 onion, chopped
- 1 teaspoon grated ginger
- Sea salt and black pepper to taste

Directions:
Set your instant pot to the sauté mode, add the coconut oil, and cook for 3-minutes. Add ginger and garlic, and cook for an additional 1-minute. Stir the remaining ingredients, close the lid, and select Manual, and cook for 10-minutes. Allow the pressure to release using the quick-release. Blend the soup with a hand blender. Divide into serving bowls. Serve warm!

Nutritional Information per serving:
Calories: 236   Fat: 9g   Carbs: 35g   Protein: 8g

Parsnip Soup
Cooking Time: 15 minutes
Servings: 4
Ingredients:
- 4 parsnips, chopped
- 4 cups vegetable stock
- Juice from 1 lemon
- ½ teaspoon chili powder

- 2 garlic cloves, crushed
- 2 tablespoons coconut oil
- 1 red onion, finely chopped
- Sea salt and black pepper to taste

Directions:
Set your instant pot to the sauté mode, add the coconut oil and heat it up. Add the parsnips, onions, garlic, and cook for 5-minutes, or until softened. Add the chili powder, and stir constantly for a few seconds. Stir in the stock, lemon juice, and lock the lid securely in place. Select the Manual setting, and cook on high for 5-minutes. To release the pressure, use the quick-release. Transfer to a food processor, and blend until smooth. Return the soup to the instant pot and set on warm for 2-minutes. Season with salt and black pepper. Divide among serving bowls. Serve warm!

Nutritional Information per serving:
Calories: 110   Fat: 7.3g   Carbs: 11g   Protein: 1.7g

Turkey & Carrot Soup
Cook Time: 15 minutes   **Servings:** 3

Ingredients:
- 5-ounces of turkey breast, chopped into pieces
- 2 carrots, sliced
- 3 cups chicken broth
- 2 tablespoons cilantro, chopped
- Sea salt and white pepper to taste

Directions:
Add all the ingredients into your instant pot and secure the lid. Press the Manual mode and set for a cook time of 35-minutes. Release the pressure naturally for 15-minutes. Divide among serving bowls. Serve hot!

Nutritional Information per serving:
Calories: 116   Fat: 2.5g   Carbs: 9g   Protein: 15g

Fish Soup
Cook Time: 45 minutes   **Servings:** 4

Ingredients:
- 6-ounces of mackerel fillets
- 4 cups fish stock
- 1 teaspoon rosemary, fresh, chopped
- ½ lb. tomatoes, peeled, diced
- ¼ cup sweet corn
- ½ cup wheat groats, soaked
- ½ cup kidney beans, soaked
- 2 tablespoons olive oil
- Sea salt and pepper to taste

Directions:
Grease the stainless-steel insert for your instant pot with olive oil. Press the sauté mode and add the tomatoes. Cook for 4-minutes, stir occasionally. Add the rosemary, fish stock, corn, wheat groats, beans, a pinch of salt. Close the lid and set the steam release handle. Press Manual and set for a cook time of 30-minutes. To release pressure, use the quick-release. Open the lid and add the mackerel fillets. Close lid again and press the Fish button, and cook for 10-minutes.

Asparagus & Sour Cream Soup
Cook Time: 25 minutes
Servings: 4
Ingredients:
- 2 lbs. asparagus, chopped
- 8-ounces sour cream
- 1 onion, chopped
- 5 cups bone broth
- 2 garlic cloves, minced
- 3 tablespoons butter
- ½ teaspoon thyme
- Salt and black pepper to taste

Directions:
Set your instant pot to the sauté mode, add the butter and heat it. Add the onions and cook for 3-minutes. Add the thyme and garlic, cook for an additional minute. Stir in the asparagus, broth, salt, pepper, and stir. Close the lid and select Manual, cook on high for 5-minutes. Allow the pressure to release naturally for 10-minutes. Stir in the sour cream. Divide among serving bowls. Serve warm!

Nutritional Information per serving:
Calories: 317 Fat: 5.6g Carbs: 16g Protein: 13g

Turkey & Black Bean Soup
Cook Time: 55 minutes
Servings: 4
Ingredients:
- 6-ounces turkey, chopped
- 1 cup black beans, dried
- 1 onion, chopped
- 1 garlic clove, minced
- 3 cups water
- 1 carrot, chopped
- ½ tablespoon olive oil
- Sea salt and black pepper to taste

Directions:
Set your instant pot to the sauté mode, and add the oil and heat. Add the onions, and carrots for 5-minutes. Add the garlic and cook for one minute more. Stir in the remaining ingredients, except the salt and pepper. Close the lid, select Manual, setting and cook on high for 45-minutes. Allow the pressure to release naturally for 10-minutes. Season with salt and pepper. Divide into serving bowls. Serve hot!

Nutritional Information per serving:
Calories: 90 Fat: 8g Carbs: 13g Protein: 10g

Brussels Sprouts Soup
Cook Time: 35 minutes
Servings: 4
Ingredients:
- 1lb. Brussels sprouts, halved, chopped
- 8-ounce baby spinach, torn chopped
- 4 tablespoons sour cream
- 1 cup milk
- 2 cups water
- 1 tablespoon celery, chopped
- 1 tablespoon butter
- ½ teaspoon Truvia
- Sea salt and black pepper to taste

Directions:
Combine all the ingredients in the instant pot. Secure the lid, and select the Soup setting and cook for 35-minutes on high pressure. Release the pressure using quick-release. Transfer the soup to a food processor and blend.
Nutritional Information per serving:
Calories: 191   Fat: 10g   Carbs: 22g   Protein: 10g

Chicken & Spinach Soup
Cook Time: 5 minutes   **Servings: 6**
Ingredients:
- 1 lb. chicken, cut into chunks
- 4 scallions, chopped
- ½ onion, chopped
- 1 bulb fennel, chopped
- 2 cups chicken broth
- 1 cup spinach
- 3 garlic cloves, minced
- Sea salt and black pepper

Directions:
Place all the ingredients into your instant pot. Select Soup, and cook for 30-minutes. Allow pressure to release naturally for 10-minutes. Divide into serving bowls. Serve warm!
Nutritional Information per serving:
Calories: 181   Fat: 3g   Carbs: 6g   Protein: 25g

Tomato Soup
Cook Time: 30 minutes   **Servings: 4**
Ingredients:
- 1 ½ lbs. tomatoes, diced
- 1 cup white beans, cooked
- 2 tablespoons sour cream
- 2 tablespoons extra virgin olive oil
- 1 garlic clove, minced
- 1 onion, diced
- 1 tablespoon parsley, fresh, chopped
- ½ cup vegetable broth
- ½ teaspoon Truvia
- Sea salt and black pepper to taste

Directions:
Set your instant pot to the sauté mode, add the oil, and heat it. Add the garlic and chopped onion, cook for 2-minutes. Add the white beans, tomatoes, vegetable broth, 2 cups water, parsley, Truvia, salt and pepper. Press the Soup setting and cook for 25-minutes on high pressure. Release the pressure naturally for 10-minutes. Top with 2 tablespoons of sour cream and parsley prior to serving. Serve warm!
Nutritional Information per serving:
Calories: 319   Fat: 16g   Carbs: 35g   Protein: 13g

Chicken Soup with Noodles
Cook Time: 40 minutes   **Servings: 4**
Ingredients:
- 1 lb. chicken meat, cut in pieces
- 4 cups chicken broth
- ½ cup soup noodles
- Parsley for garnish

- Sea salt and black pepper to taste
- 1 cup of baby spinach, chopped
- 1 large carrot, peeled, sliced

Directions:
Sprinkle the chicken bites with salt, and place them into the instant pot. Pour the chicken broth, over the chicken, carrot, spinach, and close the lid. Set the steam release handle. Press Soup and cook for 20-minutes. Press the Cancel and release the pressure naturally for 10-minutes. Add the soup noodles and cook for 5 more minutes on the Soup setting. Release the pressure again naturally for 10-minutes. Divide into serving bowls. Add black pepper and parsley for garnish. Serve hot!

Nutritional Information per serving:
Calories: 285   Fat: 11g   Carbs: 7g   Protein: 38g

Creamy Sausage & Kale Soup

Cook Time: 25 minutes
Servings: 6

Ingredients:
- 1 lb. Italian sausage, sliced
- 3 potatoes, cubed
- 1 onion, chopped
- 1 cup heavy cream
- 2 cups kale, chopped
- ¼ cup water
- 4 garlic cloves, minced
- 1 ½ cups chicken broth
- 4 bacon slices, chopped
- 1 tablespoon olive oil

Directions:
Set your instant pot to the sauté mode, add the oil and heat it. Add the bacon and cook until crispy. Transfer to a plate. Add the onions to your instant pot and cook for 3-minutes. Add the garlic and cook for 1 more minute. Add the sausage and cook for 3 more minutes. Stir in potatoes, water and kale. Close the lid and select the Manual setting and cook for 3-minutes on high pressure. Release the pressure naturally for 10-minutes. Stir in the heavy cream, and season with salt and pepper. Divide into serving bowls. Serve warm!

Nutritional Information per serving:
Calories: 500   Fat: 35g   Carbs: 35g   Protein: 28g

Lentils & Tomato Soup

Cook Time: 15 minutes
Servings: 4

Ingredients:
- 4 cups vegetable broth
- 1 medium-sized onion, chopped
- ½ teaspoon thyme, dried, ground
- 1 tablespoon parsley, chopped
- 1 carrot, thinly sliced
- 2 tomatoes, wedged
- 2 cups lentils, soaked overnight, drained
- 3 garlic cloves, peeled, crushed
- 3 tablespoons tomato paste
- ½ teaspoon cumin, ground
- Pinch of salt and black pepper

Directions:

Combine all the ingredients in your instant pot. Set the instant pot on the Manual setting, and cook on high for 8-minutes. Release the pressure naturally for 10-minutes. Divide into serving bowls. Serve warm.

Nutritional Information per serving:
Calories: 326   Fat: 3g   Carbs: 26g   Protein: 35g

Mixed Veggie Soup
Cook Time: 25 minutes   ***Servings:*** 6
Ingredients:
- 12-ounces green beans
- ¼ cup parsley, chopped
- 1 can of tomatoes, diced
- 12-ounces frozen veggies
- 2 cups veggie broth
- 2 teaspoons olive oil
- 1 teaspoon thyme
- 1 teaspoon oregano
- 2 garlic cloves, minced
- Salt and pepper to taste

Directions:
Set your instant pot to the sauté mode, add the oil and heat it. Add the onion and cook for 3-minutes. Add the thyme, garlic, oregano, and cook for another minute. Stir in the remaining ingredients. Close the lid and set to Manual setting, cook on high for 5-minutes. Allow the pressure to release naturally for 10-minutes. Divide among serving bowls. Serve hot!

Nutritional Information per serving:
Calories: 94   Fat: 3g   Carbs: 14g   Protein: 7g

Pork Soup
Cook Time: 55 minutes   ***Servings:*** 4
Ingredients:
- 4 pork chops with bones
- 2 tablespoons soy sauce
- 1 tablespoon cayenne pepper
- 1 teaspoon chili and garlic powder
- 2 tablespoons olive oil
- 2 celery stalks, diced
- 2 onions, diced
- 2 bay leaves
- 3 medium carrots, sliced

Directions:
Set your instant pot to the sauté mode, add the oil and heat it. Add the onions, cook for 3-minutes. Add the carrots, celery, chili pepper, and cook for another 8-minutes and give it a good stir. Press the Keep Warm/Cancel button then add the pork chops, garlic powder, bay leaves, and soy sauce. Pour in the broth, and seal the lid. Set to Manual mode for 35-minutes. Release the pressure using the quick-release. Divide among serving bowls. Serve warm!

Nutritional Information per serving:
Calories: 259   Fat: 52g   Carbs: 29g   Protein: 47g

Sweet Potato, Carrot & Turmeric Soup
Cook Time: 35 minutes **Servings: 4**
Ingredients:
- 3 cups veggie broth
- 2 sweet potatoes, chopped
- 3 carrots, sliced
- 2 garlic cloves, minced
- ½ teaspoon paprika
- 1 tablespoon olive oil
- 1 onion, diced
- Salt and pepper to taste

Directions:
Set your instant pot to the sauté mode, add the oil and heat it. Heat the oil and cook your onions, garlic, carrots for 3-minutes. Stir in the remaining ingredients. Close the lid and set to the Manual mode, and cook on high for 20-minutes. Release the pressure using the quick-release. Blend the soup with a hand blender. Divide among serving bowls. Serve warm!

Nutritional Information per serving:
Calories: 100   Fat: 3g   Carbs: 17g   Protein: 4g

Creamy Bean Soup
Cook Time: 20 minutes **Servings: 4**
Ingredients:
- 4 cups beef broth
- 1 cup white beans, cooked
- 1 potato, chopped
- 1 teaspoon garlic powder
- 1/3 cup heavy cream
- Sea salt and black pepper

Directions:
Add all the ingredients and cook on Manual setting for 10-minutes on high. Release the pressure naturally for 10-minutes. Transfer to food processor and blend until smooth. Return the soup to the clean stainless-steel insert and add half cup of water. Cook on sauté mode for 5-minutes. Divide among serving bowls. Serve warm!

Nutritional Information per serving:
Calories: 175   Fat: 8g   Carbs: 16g   Protein: 7.9g

Cauliflower Soup
Cook Time: 45 minutes **Servings: 4**
Ingredients:
- 1 lb. cauliflower, chopped into florets
- 4 cups chicken broth
- 1 potato, cubed
- 1 cup milk
- ¼ cup sour cream
- ½ teaspoon salt and pepper
- Parsley, fresh, chopped for garnish
- ¼ cup cooking cream

Directions:
Add the vegetables to your instant pot, add the chicken broth. Close the lid and press the Manual setting and cook on high for 20-minutes. To release the pressure, use the quick-release. Transfer to food processor and pulse until smooth. Pour back into the instant pot, add remaining ingredients. Cook on Manual for 5-minutes. Release pressure again using

quick-release. Add to serving bowls, top with fresh, chopped parsley for garnish. Serve warm!

Nutritional Information per serving:
Calories: 167   Fat: 7g   Carbs: 20g   Protein: 12g

Garlicky Leek & Potato Soup
Cook Time: 45 minutes
Servings: 4
Ingredients:

- 4 potatoes, diced
- 1 ½ teaspoons oregano
- 3 leeks, sliced
- 1 ½ cups of half and half
- 2 bay leaves
- 4 garlic cloves, minced
- 4 thyme sprigs
- 5 cups veggie broth
- 2 tablespoons butter
- Sea salt and black pepper to taste
- ¾ cup dry white wine

Directions:
Set your instant pot to the sauté mode, add the butter and heat it. Add the garlic and cook for 1-minute. Stir in the wine, broth, bay leaves, oregano, thyme, and potatoes. Close the lid and select the Manual setting and cook on high for 10-minutes. Release the pressure naturally for 10-minutes. Stir in the half and half and blend with hand blender until smooth. Divide into serving bowls. Serve warm!

Nutritional Information per serving:
Calories: 198   Fat: 9g   Carbs: 21g   Protein: 7g

Bean Soup with Chili
Cook Time: 35 minutes
Servings: 4
Ingredients:

- 15-ounces of red kidney beans, rinsed
- 14-ounce can of tomatoes
- 1 green bell pepper, diced
- ½ teaspoon Truvia
- 1 clove garlic, minced
- 1/3 cup tomato pasta sauce
- 2 ½ tablespoons olive oil
- 2 fresh red chilies, finely chopped

Directions:
Set your instant pot to the sauté mode, add the oil and heat it. Add the chili, garlic, and onion, stir and cook for 3-minutes. Add the remaining ingredients, then secure the lid to instant pot. Press the Manual setting, and cook on high-pressure for 25-minutes. Release the pressure naturally for 10-minutes. Divide into serving bowls. Serve hot!

Nutritional Information per serving:
Calories: 195   Fat: 8g   Carbs: 25g   Protein: 7g

Chapter 8. Grain Recipes

Chicken & Wild Rice Soup
Cook Time: 56 minutes
Servings: 4
Ingredients:
- 1 lb. chicken breasts, skinless, boneless, cut in half
- 4 carrots, peeled, chopped
- 2 egg yolks
- 4 cups chicken broth, divided
- 1 bay leaf
- 1 cup water
- 1 large zucchini, chopped
- ¾ cup wild rice-brown rice blend
- ½ teaspoon thyme, dried
- 1 tablespoon butter
- 2 tablespoons garlic-infused olive oil
- 1 small leek, green parts, sliced
- 3 tablespoons lemon juice
- Sea salt and black pepper to taste
- Parmesan cheese, grated for garnish
- Italian parsley, fresh, chopped for garnish

Directions:
Set your instant pot to the sauté mode, add the oil and heat it. Sauté the leek, in oil, seasoned with salt and pepper for 6-minutes. Place the chicken breasts on a cutting board to rest for a few minutes
Shred the chicken and add to the instant pot and brown meat on all sides for 5-minutes. Transfer chicken and leek to a bowl. Whisk the egg yolks, and pour in ½ a cup of chicken broth, whisking to temper the yolks. Add the yolk mixture to the instant pot along with the rest of the ingredients and stir. Return the shredded chicken and leeks to the instant pot and secure the lid. Set on Manual setting on high with a cook time of 45-minutes. Divide among serving bowls, and garnish with grated parmesan and fresh, chopped Italian parsley. Serve hot!

Nutritional Information per serving:
Calories: 227   Fat: 1g   Fiber: 2g   Carbs: 24g   Protein: 16g

Quinoa Beef Pot
Cook Time: 20 minutes
Servings: 1
Ingredients:
- 2 tablespoons of any quinoa, rinsed
- 2 tablespoons cheddar cheese, diced
- 2 tablespoons baby spinach, fresh, chopped
- 2 tablespoons beef, shredded. cooked
- 1 tablespoon ghee, melted
- Grated peel of ½ a lime and a dash of its juice
- 1 fluid ounce of water
- Sea salt and black pepper to taste

Directions:
Before cooking, rinse the quinoa under running water, until it is clear. Pour the quinoa, salt, water, and lime zest into the instant pot. Close the instant pot lid, and press the Manual button, and set it for 1-minute of pressure cooking. When the cooking is done, release the pressure naturally for 10-minutes. Add some lime juice, ghee, shredded beef, pepper,

cheese, spinach and mix. You can serve it at room temperature or you may decide to serve it at room temperature or place it in the fridge to cool before serving.
Nutritional Information per serving:
Calories: 636   Fat: 61g   Carbs: 9g   Protein: 14g

Keto Clam Chowder
Cook Time: 20 minutes   Servings: 2
Ingredients:
- 4 tablespoons of clams
- The juice contained from the clam jar in addition to water
- 2 tablespoons bacon, diced
- 4 tablespoons heavy cream
- 2 tablespoons of flour
- 2 tablespoons ghee
- 2 tablespoons butter
- 4 tablespoons sour cream
- 1 pinch of cayenne pepper, crushed
- 1 pinch of thyme, dried
- 1 bay leaf
- 4 tablespoons white wine
- 4 tablespoons onion, finely chopped

Directions:
Set your instant pot to the sauté mode, add the ghee and heat it. Add the bacon, without the lid. When the bacon begins to release fat and starts to sizzle, add the salt, pepper, onion, and cook for 5-minutes and stir. Add the wine into the instant pot once the onion has dried and stir. Allow the wine to evaporate almost completely, add the thyme, bay leaf, and cayenne pepper.
Close the lid on the instant pot and set to Manual on high for a 5-minute cook time. Release the pressure naturally for 10-minutes. Prepare the roux that will thicken the clam chowder in a pan over a low flame. Mix in the flour with butter, stirring constantly with a wooden spoon until it thickens. Add the roux, heavy cream, sour cream, add drain the clams and set them in a bowl. Set the instant pot on sauté mode and cook the ingredients for 5-minutes, stirring constantly. Then add the clams back in and stir well. Divide into serving bowls. Serve warm!
Nutritional Information per serving:
Calories: 580   Fat: 47g   Carbs: 12g   Protein: 25g

Stuffed Cuttlefish
Cook Time: 20 minutes   Servings: 3
Ingredients:
- 3 small cuttlefish, cleaned
- 2 tablespoons of shallot, chopped
- 1 tablespoon of tomato sauce
- 2 tablespoons of olive oil

For the Dip:
- 1 tablespoon anise seeds
- 1 pinch of chili powder
- 1 pinch of parsley, dried
- 2 tablespoons of flour
- 2 bay leaves
- 2 tablespoons water
- 2 tablespoons of mayonnaise

Directions:
Add all the ingredients in a mixer, except the sauce, bay leaves, water, and cuttlefish. Make the mixture homogenous. Take the cuttlefish and fill with the mixture. Put the sauce on the bottom of the instant pot, add some salt, bay leaves. Add the cuttlefish and water. Close the lid to instant pot, set to the Manual setting for 10-minutes cook time. In the meantime, prepare the dip by combining the ingredients in a small bowl. Release the pressure use the quick-release. Divide among serving plates, drizzle the sauce over fish and serve with dip. Serve warm!

Nutritional Information per serving:
Calories: 590   Fat: 47.92 g   Carbs: 10g   Protein: 27g

Saffron Chicken
Cook Time: 14 minutes   **Servings:** 2
Ingredients:

- 1 lb. chicken, skinless, boneless, cut into small strips
- 3 tablespoons olive oil
- 2 tablespoons flour
- 1 teaspoon saffron
- 1 pinch of sea salt
- 1 teaspoon rosemary needles
- 2 tablespoons of cocoa butter
- 2 tablespoons of white onion, diced
- 4 tablespoons water
- 2 teaspoons of triple tomato concentrate

Directions:
Cover the chicken strips with the flour. Set your instant pot to the sauté mode, add the oil to pot and heat it. Brown the chicken strips on all sides for 5-minutes. Add water, salt and saffron and stir. Close the lid and set to Manual setting on high with a cook time of 14-minutes. Release the pressure naturally for 10-minutes. Remove the chicken from pot, set to sauté mode to reduce the sauce. Smear the cocoa butter over the chicken. Divide among serving plates, and drizzle with sauce. Serve warm!

Nutritional Information per serving:
Calories: 713   Fat: 63g   Carbs: 9g   Protein: 36g

Sesame Meatball Stew
Cook Time: 30 minutes   **Servings:** 2
Ingredients:
For the Meatballs:

- 1 tablespoon cheddar cheese, grated
- 2 tablespoons of zucchini, grated
- 1 small egg
- 1 pinch of fresh basil, chopped
- 2 tablespoons olive oil

For the Stew:

- 1 clove of garlic, minced
- 4 tablespoons tomato sauce
- 1 tablespoon of sesame seeds
- 4 tablespoons flour
- 4 tablespoons mozzarella cheese
- Dash of salt
- 1 tablespoon parsley, dried
- ½ small onion, finely chopped

Directions:
Grate the zucchini, and add a little salt in a bowl, and flour, mix. Add the egg and grated cheddar cheese and mix well. Cut the mozzarella into cubes. Take a little of the zucchini dough and form a meatball, add three cubes of mozzarella into the middle. Add the sesame seeds, parsley in a small bowl. Roll the zucchini meatball in the sesame seeds.
Prepare a baking sheet with baking paper and place the meatballs on top of it. Sprinkle the meatballs with olive oil and bake at 400° Fahrenheit for 20-minutes. Pour the tomato sauce, garlic, and onion into your instant pot. Add the meatballs and stir. Set to the Meat/Stew setting for 10-minutes. Release the pressure naturally for 10-minutes. Divide among serving plates, drizzle with sauce. Serve warm!
Nutritional Information per serving:
Calories: 696   Fat: 140g   Carbs: 15g   Protein: 18g

Burrito with Chili Colorado
Cook Time: 40 minutes
Servings: 2
Ingredients:
- 4 tablespoons of scaled cheese
- 1 cup of water
- 4 teaspoons meat broth

For the Tortillas:
- 2 tablespoons of ghee
- 1 pinch of baking powder
- 4 tablespoons of water

- 4 tablespoons of enchilada sauce
- 1 cup roasted beef chops, boneless, cubed

- 4 tablespoons of coconut flour
- 1 egg white

Directions:
First to prepare your tortillas: Add the egg whites, coconut flour, baking powder, ghee, and water in a mixing bowl. Mix well. Heat a skillet (the size that you want your tortillas to be) on low heat. Wait until the skillet is hot, spray it with cooking spray, and drop some of the mix into the center. Tilt the skillet to spread the batter as thin as possible. Allow it to cook for a few minutes, until it starts to rise/bubble then flip it over to the other side. Flip and cook for an additional minute. Repeat the process until you have used up all the batter.
Prepare the stuffing: In your instant pot add the beef, half of the enchilada sauce, broth, and water, stir. Press the Manual setting and set for a cook time of 30-minutes. Release the pressure naturally for 10-minutes. Place the tortillas on an aluminum coated baking pan adding some beef to center of tortilla, fold the ends upwards and roll into a burrito. Repeat with other tortillas, sprinkle tops with the remaining enchilada sauce, and cheese shavings. Grill until cheese bubbles for about 4-minutes.
Nutritional Information per serving:
Calories: 502   Fat: 67g   Carbs: 8.96g   Protein: 33.82g

Sour Dumplings

Cook Time: 45 minutes **Servings:** 4

Ingredients:
- ½ cup sour cream
- 1 cup broth
- 4 tablespoons coconut oil
- 4 tablespoons tomato paste
- Salt and black pepper to taste
- 4 tablespoons of coconut flour
- 2 cloves of garlic, minced
- 1 small onion, minced
- 2 eggs
- 2 strips of bacon, minced
- 1 lb. ground pork

Directions:
In a mixing bowl mix the bacon, egg, onion, flour, seasonings, and garlic. Shape into small balls and place on a flat surface. Set your instant pot to the sauté mode, add the coconut oil and heat it. Place the meatballs into the pot, evenly spaced. Cook for 5-minutes, browning all sides of meatballs. Once they are browned remove them and set them on a plate. Add broth to pot, add meatballs back into pot. Close the lid and set pot on Manual setting for 7-minutes. After cook time is complete, release the pressure using the quick-release. Remove the meatballs from pot. Set instant pot back on to sauté mode. Add the sour cream, salt and pepper and stir the pots contents. Allow the to heat for 2-minutes. Add the meatballs back into the sauce and stir. Remove meatballs and sauce and place in bowls. Serve warm.

Nutritional Information per serving:
Calories: 608   Fat: 45g   Carbs: 12g   Protein: 41g

Sausage Radish Cakes

Cook Time: 42 minutes **Servings:** 2

Ingredients:
- ½ cup Chinese radish, peeled and chopped, cooked
- 1 teaspoon ginger, chopped
- 2 tablespoons of olive oil
- ½ cup of sausage, drained, minced
- 4 tablespoons coconut flour
- 1 cup water
- 1 cup chicken broth
- 2 tablespoons spring onions, chopped
- Pinch of salt

Directions:
Set your instant pot to the sauté mode, add the oil and heat it. Add the ginger, spring onions, and chopped sausage and cook for 5-minutes stirring often. Add the chopped Chinese radishes, and brown for 2-minutes. In a bowl mix the flour and water. Add mixture from instant pot into mixing bowl with flour and water. Add mix into a small oven-dish. Add trivet to instant pot, add the water. Place the oven-dish onto the trivet, set instant pot to Steam for 35-minutes. Release the pressure naturally for 10-minutes. Remove the steamed radish cake from instant pot. Allow for it to cool and refrigerate for a few hours. Serve room temperature.

Nutritional Information per serving:
Calories: 692   Fat: 60g   Carbs: 10g   Protein: 26g

Seafood Jambalaya
Cook Time: 45 minutes
Servings: 4
Ingredients:
- 4-ounces cod, chopped
- 4-ounces shrimp, peeled, deveined
- 1 cup brown rice, cooked
- 1 cup chicken broth
- ½ teaspoon cumin, ground
- 1 tablespoon parsley, chopped
- Sea salt and black pepper to taste
- 1 lb. Roma tomatoes, peeled, crushed
- 1 cup Russet potatoes, chopped
- ¼ cup yellow onion, diced
- ½ teaspoon cayenne pepper
- 2 teaspoons paprika, ground
- ¼ cup carrots, chopped
- 6 ½-ounces of crab meat

Directions:
Combine all ingredients in your instant pot, and cook on Meat/Stew setting for 45-minutes. Divide into serving bowls, garnish with fresh chopped parsley. Serve hot!

Nutritional Information per serving:
Calories: 137   Fat: 2g   Carbs: 13g   Protein: 20g

Shredded Pork Fajitas
Cook Time: 40 minutes
Servings: 4
Ingredients:
- 1lb. stewing pork, chopped
- 8 whole-wheat fajitas
- ½ small onion, sliced
- 1 green pepper, diced
- 1 jalapeno, minced
- 1 tablespoon olive oil
- ½ teaspoon cumin, ground
- Sea salt and black pepper to taste
- 2 cloves garlic, minced

Directions:
Combine all the ingredients in your instant pot, except the fajitas. Cook on Manual setting for 40-minutes on high. Release the pressure naturally for 10-minutes. Remove the pork to a cutting board and shred it with two forks, then add back to the instant pot and stir. Place fajitas on serving plates and top with pork mix from instant pot and roll up. Serve warm!

Nutritional Information per serving:
Calories: 238   Fat: 17g   Carbs: 18g   Protein: 21g

Sausage Gumbo

Cook Time: 35 minutes
Servings: 6
Ingredients:
- 8-ounces, Andouille sausage, whole
- 4 cups pork stock
- 1 cup of brown rice, cooked
- 1 tablespoon thyme, fresh, chopped
- ½ teaspoon ginger, ground
- ½ teaspoon cumin, ground
- ½ teaspoon cayenne pepper, ground
- 1 teaspoon paprika, ground
- Sea salt and black pepper to taste
- 2 cups Roma tomatoes, peeled and diced
- ¼ cup yellow onion, sliced

Directions:
Combine all the ingredients in your instant pot, except the brown rice. Cook on Manual setting on high for a cook time of 35-minutes. Release the pressure naturally for 10-minutes. Add in the cooked brown rice and mix well. Spoon into serving bowls, topped with fresh chopped thyme for garnish. Serve warm!

Nutritional Information per serving:
Calories: 118   Fat: 4g   Carbs: 13g   Protein: 10g

Pork Fried Whole Grain Rice

Cooking Time: 45 minutes
Servings: 4
Ingredients:
- 1lb. stewing pork, diced
- 1 tablespoon green onion, chopped
- 2 eggs, scrambled
- ½ teaspoon ginger, ground
- ½ teaspoon cumin, ground
- 1 clove garlic, minced
- 1 teaspoon rice vinegar
- 2 cups whole grain rice, cooked
- ¼ cup green beans, diced
- ¼ cup carrots, diced
- ¼ cup yellow onion, diced

Directions:
Add all the ingredients to your instant pot, except for eggs and green onion. Cook on Manual setting for 45-minutes. Release the pressure naturally for 10-minutes. Stir in the scrambled eggs and green onions. Divide among serving dishes. Serve warm!

Nutritional Information per serving:
Calories: 218   Fat: 16g   Carbs: 24g   Protein: 21g

Bacon Wrapped Jalapenos

Cook Time: 32 minutes
Servings: 4
Ingredients:
- 12 large jalapenos
- 6 slices of bacon
- ½ teaspoon salt
- ½ tablespoon olive oil
- ½ red bell pepper, diced
- ½ cup brown rice, cooked

Directions:

Slice the tops off the jalapenos, then take a spoon to remove and scoop out the seeds. Set the hollowed jalapenos aside. In a mixing bowl, combine the cooked brown rice, olive oil, bell pepper, and salt. Stuff the mixture into each jalapeno. Slice each piece of bacon in half longways, and wrap one slice around each jalapeno, use toothpick to hold in place. Place the wrapped jalapenos gently inside your instant pot. Cook on Manual setting for 32-minutes. Release the pressure naturally for 15-minutes. Divide among serving plates. Serve warm!

Nutritional Information per serving:
Calories: 187   Fat: 18g   Carbs: 12g   Protein: 14g

Shredded Beef Tacos
Cook Time: 35 minutes　　　　　　　　　　*Servings: 2*
Ingredients:

- 6-ounces beef tenderloin, chopped
- 4 taco shells
- 1 jalapeno, diced
- ½ red bell pepper, sliced
- 1 tsp. red wine vinegar
- ½ tsp. cumin, ground
- 2 cloves garlic, minced
- Salt and black pepper to taste

Directions:
Combine all your ingredients in your instant pot, except for the taco shells. Set your instant pot to the Manual setting on a high cook time of 35-minutes. Once the cook time is completed, release the pressure naturally for 10-minutes. Shred the beef with a pair of forks. Scoop the mixture into the taco shells and serve warm.

Nutritional Information per serving:
Calories: 299   Fat: 21g   Carbs: 13g   Protein: 22g

Beef Stuffed Eggplant
Cooking Time: 35 minutes　　　　　　　　*Servings: 4*
Ingredients:

- 1 tablespoon olive oil
- ¼ cup yellow onion, diced
- ½ cup brown rice
- ½ tablespoon mint, fresh, chopped
- 1 tablespoon basil, fresh, chopped
- Sea salt and black pepper to taste
- 8-ounces lean ground beef, browned
- 1 eggplant, cut in half vertically and horizontally (4-pieces)

Directions:
Scoop out the insides of the eggplant using a spoon. Leave each piece with a ½-inch thick wall. Dice the removed fruit. Combine the diced eggplant with the remaining ingredients (except the olive oil) in a mixing bowl. Fill each eggplant slice with the mixture. Place the stuffed eggplants into your instant pot, and drizzle with olive oil over each piece. Set to Manual setting for a cook time of 35-minutes. When cooking is completed, release the pressure naturally for 10-minutes. Divide among serving plates. Serve warm!

Nutritional Information per serving:
Calories: 284   Fat: 12g   Carbs: 26g   Protein: 22g

Spicy Fire Chicken with Rice
Cook Time: 45 minutes **Servings: 2**
Ingredients:
- 8-ounces chicken breasts, skinless, boneless, chopped
- 1 red chili, diced
- 1 teaspoon crushed red pepper
- ½ teaspoon paprika, ground
- Salt and black pepper to taste
- ½ tablespoon olive oil
- 2 cups brown rice, cooked

Directions:
Combine all your ingredients in your instant pot except for the rice. Stir and set to Meat/Stew setting for 45-minutes. When the cooking is completed, release the pressure naturally for 15-minutes. Serve on top of a bed of rice the spicy fire chicken. Serve warm.

Nutritional Information per serving:
Calories: 288   Fat: 7.5g   Carbs: 13g   Protein: 40g

Spiced Apple & Walnut Chicken
Cook Time: 40 minutes **Servings: 2**
Ingredients:
- 8-ounces chicken breast, skinless, boneless, chopped
- ¼ cup walnuts, chopped
- ½ teaspoon nutmeg, ground
- ½ teaspoon ginger, ground
- 1 small apple, peeled and diced
- 1 tablespoon ghee
- Salt and black pepper to taste
- 2 cups brown rice, cooked

Directions:
Set your instant pot to the sauté mode, and add the ghee and heat it. Add the chicken to instant pot and cook for 5-minutes, browning all sides of meat. Add the remaining ingredients to pot, except cooked brown rice. Set the setting to Manual for a cook time of 35-minutes. When the cook time has completed, release the pressure naturally for 10-minutes. Serve on a bed of brown rice. Serve warm!

Nutritional Information per serving:
Calories: 296   Fat: 8g   Carbs: 18g   bProtein: 49g

Pulled Chicken in Soft Whole Wheat Tacos
Cook Time: 38 minutes **Servings: 6**
Ingredients:
- 1 lb. chicken breast, skinless, boneless, cubed
- ½ cup chicken broth
- 2 tablespoons cilantro, chopped, fresh
- ½ teaspoon cayenne pepper, ground
- Salt and black pepper to taste
- ½ teaspoon cumin
- 2 Roma tomatoes, peeled, diced
- ¼ red onion, diced
- ½ green bell pepper, sliced
- ½ red bell pepper, sliced
- ¼ yellow onion, diced

- ½ teaspoon mustard powder, ground
- 1 tablespoon coconut oil

Directions:
Set your instant pot to the sauté mode, add the coconut oil and heat it up. Add the chicken and cook for 5-minutes, stir. Add bell peppers, onion and cook for an additional 3-minutes. Add the remaining ingredients to instant pot, except the soft tacos. Secure the lid of instant pot in place, and set to Manual setting for 30-minutes on high cook time. When the cook time is complete, release the pressure naturally for 10-minutes. Spoon the chicken mix on top of soft tacos. Serve warm!

Nutritional Information per serving:
Calories: 158   Fat: 3.5g   Carbs: 17g   Protein: 25g

Pesto Chicken & Whole Wheat Pasta
Cook Time: 35 minutes   **Servings:** 2

Ingredients:
- 2 cups whole wheat pasta, cooked
- 2 chicken breasts, skinless, boneless
- 2 tablespoons pesto sauce
- 2 cloves garlic, minced
- Sal and black pepper to taste
- ½ cup of parsley, fresh, chopped for garnish

Directions:
Mix the seasonings together, then run them into each chicken breast. Place the chicken breasts inside instant pot, add a tablespoon of pesto on top of each piece of chicken. Set to Manual setting on high cook time of 35-minutes. When the cooking is completed, release the pressure naturally for 10-minutes. Serve on top of a bed of whole wheat pasta. Garnish with fresh chopped pasta. Serve warm!

Nutritional Information per serving:
Calories: 258   Fat: 6g   Carbs: 10g   Protein: 44g

Chapter 8. Egg Instant Pot Recipes

Eggs En Cocotte
Cook Time: *4 minutes* ***Servings:*** *3*

Ingredients:
- 3 eggs, fresh
- Sea salt and black pepper to taste
- 1 cup water, for the pot
- Butter, at room temperature
- 1 tablespoon of chives
- 3 tablespoons cream

Directions:
Take 3 four-ounce ramekins, and wipe the insides of them with butter applied using a paper towel. Pour 1 tablespoon of cream into each ramekin. Carefully crack an egg into each ramekin, making sure not to break the yolks. Then sprinkle with chives. Pour the water into the bottom of the instant pot and place trivet into instant pot. Place the ramekins on top of trivet. Close the instant pot and set to the Manual setting on low for a cook time of 4-minutes. When the cook time is completed, release the pressure using quick-release. Remove the ramekins from pot using a kitchen towel. Season eggs en cocotte with salt and pepper. Serve with toast. Serve warm!

Nutritional Information per serving:
Calories: 173   Fat: 9g   Carbs: 6.5g   Protein: 8.6g

Spinach & Tomato Crustless Quiche
Cook Time: *20 minutes* ***Servings:*** *6*

Ingredients:
- 12 large eggs
- ¼ teaspoon fresh ground black pepper
- 1 ½ cups water for the instant pot
- 1 cup tomato, seeded, diced
- ½ cup milk
- 4 tomato slices, for topping for quiche
- Salt as needed
- 3 large green onions, sliced
- ¼ cup Parmesan cheese, shredded
- 3 cups baby spinach, roughly chopped

Directions:
Pour the water into the instant pot. In a mixing bowl, add eggs, milk, pepper, salt and whisk. Add the tomato, spinach, and green onions into a 1 ½ quart-sized baking dish; mix well to combine. Pour the egg mixture over the vegetables, stir until well combined. Place the tomato slices gently on top. Sprinkle with shredded Parmesan cheese. Place the trivet inside instant pot, then place baking dish onto trivet. Secure the lid to instant pot, and set on the Manual setting to high with a cook time of 20-minutes. When the cook time is completed, release the pressure naturally for 10-minutes. Remove the baking dish from instant pot, can broil in oven for a few minutes to brown top if you wish. Divide among serving dishes, and serve warm!

Nutritional Information per serving:
Calories: 179   Fat: 3.8g   Carbs: 5g   Protein: 48.6g

Bacon & Cheese Egg Muffins
Cook Time: 8 minutes
Servings: 4
Ingredients:

- 4 eggs
- 4 slices bacon, cooked, crumbled
- 4 tablespoons pepper jack cheese, or cheddar
- ¼ teaspoon lemon pepper seasoning
- 1 green onion, diced
- 1 ½ cups of water for instant pot

Directions:
Add the water to your instant pot, then place a steamer basket into the pot. In a large mixing bowl, add the eggs, lemon pepper, and beat well. Divide the bacon, cheese, and green onions between 4 silicone muffin cups. Pour the egg mix into each muffin cup, stir with a fork. Put the muffins into steamer basket, cover and secure lid to instant pot. Set to Manual setting at high with a cook time of 8-minutes. Remove the steamer basket from instant pot, and serve the egg muffins right away. Serve warm!

Nutritional Information per serving:
Calories: 127   Fat: 9.4g   Carbs: 0.9g   Protein: 9.7g

Meaty Crustless Quiche
Cook Time: 30 minutes
Servings: 4
Ingredients:

- 6 large eggs, well beaten
- ½ cup milk
- 1 cup ground sausage, cooked
- 4 slices bacon, cooked and crumbled
- Salt and black pepper to taste
- 1 ½ cups water for the instant pot
- 1 cup cheese, shredded
- 2 large green onions, chopped
- ½ cup ham, diced

Directions:
Add the water to your instant pot, place a trivet into the pot. In a large mixing bowl, whisk the milk, eggs, salt and pepper. Add the sausage, cheese, ham, bacon, and green onions. Add this mix to a 1-quart soufflé dish; mix well. Pour egg mix over meat, stir to combine. Loosely cover the dish with aluminum foil. Put on to the trivet, and secure the instant pot lid into place. Set to Manual setting on high with a cook time of 30-minutes. When the cook time is completed, release the pressure naturally for 10-minutes. Remove dish from instant pot and sprinkle the top of quiche with additional cheese and broil until melted and slightly browned. Divide into serving dishes. Serve warm!

Nutritional Information per serving:
Calories: 419   Fat: 14g   Carbs: 6.5g   Protein: 29g

Breakfast in a Jar
Cook Time: 5 minutes
Servings: 3
Ingredients:
- 6 eggs
- Tater tots
- 6 pieces bacon, cooked
- 6 tablespoons peach-mango salsa, divided
- 9 slices sharp cheese, shredded, divided

Directions:
You will need three mason jars, that can hold about 2-cups worth of ingredients. Add 1 ¼ cups of water to your instant pot. Add enough tater tots to cover the bottom of mason jars. Crack 2 eggs into each mason jar. Poke the eggs using a fork. Add two bacon slices into each mason jar. Add 2 slices of cheese into each mason jar, covering the ingredients. Add 2 tablespoons of salsa into each jar, on top of cheese. Add a few more tater tots on top of salsa. Then top with a slice of cheese in each jar. Cover each jar with foil, making sure to cover them tightly to prevent moisture getting into the jars. Place the jars right into the water inside your instant pot. Cover and secure the lid, setting to Manual setting on high for a cook time of 5-minutes. When cook time is completed, release the pressure using quick-release. Remove jars carefully, transfer contents onto serving plates. Serve warm!

Nutritional Information per serving:
Calories: 632   Fat: 18g   Carbs: 15g   Protein: 38g

Bread Pudding
Cook Time: 25 minutes
Servings: 8
Ingredients:
- 6 slices of raisin bread, dried out
- 3 large eggs
- 3 cups milk
- 1 teaspoon vanilla
- 2 cups water
- 1 tablespoon butter
- Truvia to taste
- Cinnamon to taste

Directions:
In a mixing bowl add 3 cups milk, 3 eggs, 1 teaspoon vanilla, ½ teaspoon salt, Truvia to taste, cinnamon to taste. Butter a 5-cup stainless steel bowl that will fit into your instant pot. Put the cut bread pieces into the bowl. Pour the custard mix over bread and allow to stand for 15-minutes. Dot the top with 1 tablespoon of butter. Butter a piece of aluminum foil with buttered piece facing down, and tightly cover the bowl. Pour water into instant pot and then place the trivet into pot. Place the bowl on top of trivet. Secure the lid in place and set to Manual on high with a cook time of 25-minutes. When the cook time is completed, release pressure naturally for 15-minutes. Lift bowl out of instant pot, puncture the foil with a fork to allow the pudding to cool. Serve pudding warm or cold!

Nutritional Information per serving:
Calories: 152   Fat: 5.4g   Carbs: 20g   Protein: 5.9g

Boiled Eggs
Cook Time: *3 minutes*
Servings: *6*
Ingredients:
- 12 large eggs
- 1 cup water

Directions:
Add the water to your instant pot, and then place the steamer basket into pot. Place the eggs into the basket. Secure the lid on instant pot, and set to the Manual setting on low with a cook time of 3-minutes. When the cook time is completed, release the pressure using the quick-release. Serve the boiled eggs warm or cold!

Nutritional Information per serving:
Calories: 63 Fat: 4.4g Carbs: 0.3g Protein: 5.5g

Turkey Meatballs with Mushroom Gravy
Cook Time: *40 minutes*
Servings: *4*
Ingredients:
- 1 lb. ground turkey
- 1 large egg, beaten
- 1 onion, small-sized, minced
- 1 teaspoon oregano, dried
- ½ cup panko bread crumbs
- 1 teaspoon light soy sauce
- 1 teaspoon fish sauce
- 4 cloves garlic, minced
- 20 grams Parmesan cheese, freshly grated
- ¼ teaspoon Italian parsley, finely chopped
- Sea salt and black pepper to taste

For the Mushroom Gravy:
- 12 cremini mushrooms, roughly chopped
- 3 shiitake mushrooms, dried, about 14 grams, roughly chopped
- Salt and black pepper to taste
- 2 tablespoons cornstarch with 2 tablespoons cold tap water
- 1 tablespoon olive oil
- 1 cup chicken stock
- Dash of sherry wine
- 1 teaspoon light soy sauce
- 2 tablespoons butter, unsalted

Directions:
Add all the dry ingredients to a large-sized mixing bowl. Add the wet ingredients into the dry ingredients. With clean hands mix thoroughly until well combined. Roll and form about 16 meatballs from mixture. Set your instant pot to sauté mode, add the olive oil and heat. Add the meatballs into pot and stir, brown meat on all sides for about 5-minutes.
Remove the meatballs and set on a plate. Add chicken stock to pot, and scrape off brown bits from pot. Add the butter to pot, add the mushrooms, and season with pepper and salt. Stir to coat the mushrooms with cooking fat. Cook for 12-minutes, until mushrooms are brown and crisp. Add the shiitake mushrooms into pot and stir immediately. Pour a dash

of sherry into pot and stir. Add soy sauce, and meatballs back into pot. Cover the pot with lid, and press the Manual setting on high for a cook time of 6-minutes.

When the cook time is completed, release the pressure using quick-release. In a bowl mix the cornstarch with the water until dissolved. Remove meatballs from pot onto large serving plate. Add cornstarch mix into pot and mix, until the sauce reaches your desired thickness. Drizzle the mushroom gravy over meatballs, serve with mashed potatoes, pasta, cooked rice etc. Serve warm!

Nutritional Information per serving:
Calories: 112   Fat: 2g   Carbs: 12g   Protein: 6g

Cheese-Stuffed Mini Turkey Meatloaves & Mushroom Gravy
Cook Time: *25 minutes*
Servings: *4 servings*
Ingredients:
- 1 lb. ground turkey
- 4 tablespoons gournay cheese spread, such as Boursin Garlic and Fine Herbs
- 3 cups mushrooms, sliced, divided
- 2 tablespoons butter
- ½ teaspoon onion powder
- ½ teaspoon garlic powder
- ½ cup breadcrumbs, plain
- 1 teaspoon Italian seasoning
- 1 tablespoon water
- 1 tablespoon cornstarch
- 1 cup chicken broth
- 1 egg
- Salt and black pepper to taste

Directions:
Grease four mini meatloaf, disposable pans, with non-stick cooking spray. Set your instant pot to the sauté mode, add 2 tablespoons butter and heat. Add the mushrooms to pot and sauté for 5-minutes, then remove mushrooms and set on a plate. Pour broth into instant pot.

Set aside 2/3 of mushrooms for the gravy, and dice the remaining 1/3 into fine pieces. In a large mixing bowl, combine the ground turkey with diced mushroom, egg, breadcrumbs, garlic powder, onion powder, Italian seasoning, salt and pepper. Mix the ingredients with clean hands, until well combined. Divide the mixture into 4 portions and place portions into pans. Create a row in the center of each meatloaf. Fill the row with 1 tablespoon of gournay cheese. Close row by pinching it. Set a trivet into the bottom of instant pot. Add 2 meatloaf pans on top of trivet.

Place a second trivet on the first, place the remaining meatloaf pans on top of second trivet. Cover and lock the lid of instant pot, setting to Manual on high for a cook time of 12-minutes. When the cook time is completed, release pressure naturally for 15-minutes. Remove the meatloaf pans and trivets. Cover the meatloaves with foil to keep them warm. Add the reserved 2/3 mushrooms into the instant pot. In a bowl mix the cornstarch with water until dissolved. Pour into instant pot and stir until sauce thickens. Season to taste with salt and pepper. Serve the mushroom gravy over the mini cheese-stuffed meatloaves. Serve with pan roasted sweet potatoes and green beans. Serve warm!

Nutritional Information per serving:
Calories: 404   Fat: 23g   Carbs: 14g   Protein: 39g

Mushroom Stroganoff

Cook Time: 10 minutes
Servings: 4
Ingredients:

- 1 egg, large-sized, beaten
- 1 lb. ground turkey, lean
- ½ teaspoon Worcestershire sauce
- ½ teaspoon paprika
- ½ cup onion, chopped
- ½ cup sour cream, light
- 1 teaspoon olive oil, divided
- 1 sprig thyme, fresh
- 8-ounces cremini mushrooms, sliced
- Sea salt and black pepper to taste
- ¾ cup water
- 3 tablespoons milk, fat-free
- 2 teaspoons tomato paste
- 2 teaspoons beef bouillon
- 2 tablespoons all-purpose flour
- ¼ parsley, chopped, divided
- 1/3 cup seasoned breadcrumbs, whole-wheat

Directions:

Set your instant pot to the sauté mode, add ½ teaspoon olive oil and heat. Add onion and sauté for 3-minutes. Remove and divide into two portions. Turn off the instant pot. In a large mixing bowl, combine turkey, half of sautéed onions, bread crumbs, egg, milk, 2 tablespoons parsley, ¾ teaspoon black pepper, ¾ teaspoon salt, shape into meatballs.

Pour the sour cream, water, flour, Worcestershire sauce, tomato paste, bouillon and paprika into blender, blend until smooth. Set your instant pot to sauté mode, add remaining olive oil. Add half of the meatballs into pot, and brown them on all sides for about 5-minutes. Transfer the browned meatballs onto a plate and set aside. Repeat the process with remaining meatballs. After second batch is cooked add the first batch back into pot along with remaining onions. Pour the sauce over meatballs, add mushrooms and thyme. Cover and secure the lid on pot and press the Manual setting on high for 10-minutes. When the cook time is completed, release the pressure using the quick-release. Remove and discard the thyme. Add the parsley and serve over your favorite noodles. Serve warm!

Nutritional Information per serving:
Calories: 391   Fat: 21g   Carbs: 16.3g   Protein: 37.2g

Korean Style Steamed Eggs

Cook Time: 5 minutes
Servings: 1
Ingredients:

- 1 large egg
- 1/3 cup cold water
- Pinch of garlic powder
- 1 teaspoon scallions, chopped
- Salt and pepper to taste

Directions:

Mix the egg and water in a small bowl. Strain the egg mixture over a fine mesh strainer into a heat proof bowl. Add the rest of the ingredients and mix well. Add 1 cup of water to instant pot, place the trivet into pot. Place the bowl with egg mixture on top of trivet. Close and secure the lid to pot, set to the Manual setting on high for a cook time of 5-minutes. When

the cook time is completed, release the pressure using quick-release. Serve with some hot rice of your choice. Serve warm!
Nutritional Information per serving:
Calories: 114   Fat: 2g   Carbs: 9g   Protein: 6g

Eggs De Provence
Cook Time: 30 minutes   **Servings:** 6
Ingredients:
- 6 eggs
- 1/8 teaspoon sea salt and black pepper
- 1 onion, small, chopped
- 1 cup cooked ham
- ½ cup heavy cream
- 1 teaspoon Herbes de Provence
- 1 cup cheddar cheese

Directions:
Whisk the eggs with the heavy cream in a mixing bowl. Add the rest of the ingredients and combine well. Pour the mixture into a heat proof dish and cover. Add one cup of water in the instant pot. Place the trivet into the instant pot. Place the heat proof dish with egg mixture, on top of trivet. Close and secure the lid on pot, and set to Manual setting on high for a cook time of 20-minutes. Serve warm!
Nutritional Information per serving:
Calories: 109   Fat: 2.3g   Carbs: 14g   Protein: 21g

Instant Pot Poached Eggs Over Spicy Potato Hash
Cook Time: 15 minutes   **Servings:** 2
Ingredients:
- 1 cup sweet potatoes, peeled, cubed into 1-inch cubes
- 2 eggs
- 1 teaspoon taco seasoning, for garnish
- 1 tablespoon cilantro, fresh, chopped, for garnish
- 1 jalapeno pepper, sliced
- 2 tablespoons bacon fat
- 1 tablespoon bacon, cooked, chopped

Directions:
Add a cup of water to the inside of your instant pot, and place trivet inside. Place the heat proof bowl with potatoes on top of trivet. Close the lid and secure, set to Manual setting on high for 2-minutes. Meanwhile chop onions, bacon, jalapeno pepper, and cilantro. When the cook time is completed, release the pressure using the quick-release. Remove the potatoes and set aside. Remove the trivet and drain the water from instant pot. Set your instant pot to the sauté mode, add the bacon fat. Add the onions and sauté for 3-minutes. Add the potatoes, bacon, pepper and mix well. Pat down the potatoes to create a crater in the middle. Crack both eggs into the crater of the potato hash. Close the lid and set on Manual setting on high for 1-minute. Use the quick-release to release the pressure. Place carefully on serving plates and try not to break eggs yolks. Garnish with taco seasoning and cilantro. Serve warm!

Instant Pot Ham & Egg Casserole
Cook Time: 25 minutes
Servings: 5
Ingredients:
- 4 medium red potatoes
- 1 cup milk
- 10 large eggs
- 2 cups cheddar cheese, shredded
- 1 cup ham, chopped
- ½ onion, diced
- Sea salt and black pepper to taste

Directions:
Spray the insert of your instant pot with non-stick cooking spray. Add eggs and milk into a heat proof bowl, and whisk to blend. Add the potatoes, onions, cheese, ham, salt and pepper into the bowl with eggs, and whisk until well combined. Cover the bowl with foil. Place your trivet into your instant pot, and add 2 cups of water into pot. Place the bowl with egg mixture on top of the trivet. Close and secure the lid to pot, and set to Manual on high with a cook time of 25-minutes. When the cook time is completed, release the pressure using the quick-release. Serve with favorite toppings some of mine are: more cheese and tomatoes, sour cream, avocado, and salsa. Serve warm!

Nutritional Information per serving:
Calories: 172   Fat: 2g   Carbs: 27   Protein: 32g

Instant Pot Aromatic Egg
Cook Time: 20 minutes
Servings: 6
Ingredients:
- 8 eggs
- 1 tablespoon mustard
- ¼ cup cream
- 1 cup water
- 1 teaspoon minced garlic
- 1 teaspoon ground white pepper
- ¼ cup dill
- 1 teaspoon mayo sauce

Directions:
Add a cup of water to your instant pot. Add the stainless steamer basket inside the pot. Place the eggs in the steamer basket. Cook the eggs on Manual setting on high for a cook time of 5-minutes. Remove the eggs from the instant pot and allow to chill in some cold water. Peel the eggs, and cut them in half. Remove the egg yolks and mash them in a bowl. Add the mustard, cream, salt, mayo sauce, ground white pepper, and minced garlic in with mashed yolks. Sprinkle dill into the yolk mix and combine well. Put egg yolk mixture into a pastry bag. Fill the egg whites with yolk mixture. Serve cold!

Nutritional Information per serving:
Calories: 62   Fat: 1g   Carbs: 11g   Protein: 15g

Instant Pot Western Omelette Quiche
Cook Time: 30 minutes
Servings: 4
Ingredients:

- 6 large eggs, beaten
- ¼ cup cheddar cheese, shredded, for garnish
- ¾ cup cheddar cheese, shredded
- 3 spring onions, thinly sliced, reserve the tops for garnish
- ¾ cup red and green bell peppers, diced
- 8-ounces Canadian bacon, diced, cooked
- Sea salt and black pepper to taste
- ½ cup half and half
- 1 ½ cups water for instant pot

Directions:
Add the water to bottom of your instant pot, place the trivet inside pot. Spray a soufflé dish with non-stick cooking spray. In a large mixing bowl whisk together the eggs, milk, salt and pepper. Add the bacon, diced peppers, spring onion slices, cheese into 1-quart soufflé dish and combine well. Pour the egg mixture over the meat and stir to combine ingredients. Cover your soufflé dish loosely with a piece of foil. Place the lid onto instant pot and secure it in place, set to Manual setting on high with a cook time of 30-minutes. When the cooking is completed, release the pressure naturally for 10-minutes. Remove the dish from pot and remove foil, sprinkle top with cheese. Broil until lightly browned. Divide among serving plates, and garnish with chopped spring onion. Serve warm!

Nutritional Information per serving:
Calories: 365   Fat: 24g   Fiber: 1g   Carbs: 6g   Protein: 29g

Instant Pot French Baked Eggs
Cook Time: 8 minutes
Servings: 4
Ingredients:

- 4 eggs
- 4 slices of ham or favorite meat slices or veggies
- 4 slices of favorite cheese
- 4 fresh herbs, garnish
- 1 cup water for instant pot

Directions:
Add cup of water to your instant pot, and place the trivet inside. Prepare four ramekins by adding a drop of olive oil into each ramekin, rubbing sides and bottom of dish. Lay a slice of preferred meat into dish. Break an egg into ramekin, then add a slice of cheese of choice. For a soft yolk, cover tightly with tin foil, for a fully-cooked hard yolk leave uncovered. Place the ramekins into steamer basket and place on top of trivet. Close the lid and secure, set to Manual setting on low with an 8-minute cook time. When the cook time is completed, release the pressure using the quick-release. Remove ramekins and garnish with fresh herbs of choice. Serve warm!

Nutritional Information per serving:
Calories: 312   Fat: 4g   Fiber: 1g   Carbs: 9g   Protein: 21g

Instant Pot Mexican Egg Casserole
Cook Time: 25 minutes **Servings:** 8
Ingredients:
- 8 large eggs, well-beaten
- 1 cup mozzarella cheese, divided
- ½ cup almond flour
- ½ cup green onions
- 1 can black beans, rinsed
- 1 red bell pepper, chopped
- ½ large red onion, chopped
- 1 lb. ground sausage
- Sour cream, and cilantro for garnish
- 1 tablespoon olive oil
- 1 cup Cotija cheese

Directions:
Set your instant pot to the sauté mode, add oil and heat it. Add the sausage and onions, cook for about 6-minutes. In a mixing bowl mix the eggs and flour until well combined. Add the egg mixture into the instant pot with the sausage and onions. Add in the chopped vegetables, cheeses, beans to the instant pot. Set aside some mozzarella cheese to use for garnish. Secure the lid into place on instant pot, set to Manual setting on high with a cook time of 20-minutes. Remove the casserole from instant pot, add mozzarella for garnish. Serve warm!

Nutritional Information per serving:
Calories: 294   Fat: 16g   Fiber: 2g   Carbs: 21g   Protein: 23g

Eggs Papin Poached Eggs in Bell Pepper Cup
Cook Time: 10 minutes **Servings:** 2
Ingredients:
- 2 fresh eggs
- 2 red bell peppers, ends cut off
- 1 small bunch of Rucola
- 2 slices of Smoked Scamorza, Mozzarella or Gouda
- 2 slices whole wheat bread, toasted
- 1 cup of water for instant pot

For the Mock Hollandaise sauce:
- 1 teaspoon turmeric
- 1 tablespoon white wine vinegar
- 1 teaspoon fresh lemon juice
- 3 tablespoons orange juice
- 2/3 cup mayonnaise
- ½ teaspoon salt

Directions:
Make the Mock Hollandaise sauce by whisking all the ingredients until smooth, you can refrigerate over night to be used the next day. Add the cup of water to your instant pot, add trivet and steamer basket on top of trivet. Cut the bell pepper ends to form cups, then break an egg inside of the cups. Cover with foil and place inside of steamer basket. Close and lock the instant pot lid, set it to Manual setting on low with a cook time of 4-minutes. When the cook time is completed, release the pressure using quick-release. Stack toast, smoked cheese, Rucola, pepper cups, and cover with a generous dollop of mock-hollandaise sauce, and serve warm!

Egg Bake

***Cook Time:** 10 minutes* ***Servings:** 4*

Ingredients:
- 6 eggs
- ½ green bell pepper, diced
- 1 tablespoon milk
- 1/3 cup cheddar cheese shredded
- ½ red bell pepper, diced
- 2/3 cups hash browns, frozen
- Green onion, chopped, fresh, for garnish
- 1 tablespoon coconut oil

Directions:
Set your instant pot to the sauté mode, add oil and heat. Add diced peppers, hash browns and cook for 5-minutes, stir. Whisk the eggs, milk along with a pinch of salt. Pour the eggs over the pepper mixture, add the cheese and stir to combine. Secure the lid and set to high pressure and a cook time of 10-minutes. Once the cook time is completed, release the pressure naturally for 10-minutes. Divide among serving dishes, garnish with green onions. Serve warm!

Nutritional Information per serving:
Calories: 165   Fat: 20g   Fiber: 1g   Carbs: 15g   Protein: 19g

Chapter 9. Bean & Lentil Instant Pot Recipes

Mung Bean Dahl
Cook Time: 25 minutes
Servings: 6
Ingredients:
- ½ cup mung beans, dry
- 2 teaspoons curry powder
- 2 cups vegetable stock
- ½ teaspoon onion powder
- ¼ teaspoon garlic powder
- Salt and black pepper to taste
- 1 cup spinach, chopped finely

Directions:
Add the stock, curry powder, mung beans, onion and garlic powder into instant pot with some salt. Secure the pot lid in place, and set on Manual setting for a cook time of 25-minutes. When the cook time is completed, release the pressure naturally for 10-minutes. Using a fork, smash about the beans and stir to thicken sauce. Add the spinach and stir allowing it cook within the residual heat. Serve warm!

Nutritional Information per serving:
Calories: 203   Fat: 7g   Fiber: 1g   Carbs: 6g   Protein: 8g

Red Bean & Lentil Chili
Cook Time: 38 minutes
Servings: 6
Ingredients:
- ½ cup red beans, dried, soaked in water overnight
- ½ cup brown lentils, soaked in water overnight
- 1 teaspoon cumin powder
- ½ teaspoon coriander powder
- 1 ½ teaspoons chili powder
- 1 teaspoon smoked paprika
- 5 cloves garlic, minced
- 1 green bell pepper, chopped
- 1 cup carrot, chopped
- ½ cup yellow onion, chopped
- 1 cup frozen corn
- ¼ cup tomato paste
- 14.5 ounce can of tomatoes, diced
- 2 tablespoons soy sauce
- ½ teaspoon cayenne pepper
- ½ teaspoon allspice
- ½ teaspoon oregano, dried
- 1 ½ cups water

Directions:
Soak the beans and lentils in water overnight. When you are ready to cook your chili, rinse and drain the beans and lentils in a fine mesh strainer, then set aside for now. Get all your veggies prepped and measure out all your spices for your chili. Set your instant pot on the sauté mode, and allow it to heat up for 2-minutes. Add the onion, bell pepper, carrot, and garlic and sauté for 5-minutes, stir occasionally.   Add in the smoked paprika, coriander powder, chili powder, dried oregano, cumin powder, cayenne, allspice, soy sauce, diced tomatoes, salt, tomato paste, lentils and red beans, stir to combine ingredients. Cook and stir for about a minute then add in the water and stir once more. Secure the lid to pot in place, set it to Manual setting on high with a cook time of 30-minutes. When the cooking is

completed, release the pressure using natural release of 15-minutes. Add the corn and stir. Divide among serving bowls, and serve hot!
Nutritional Information per serving:
Calories: 206   Fat: 8g   Fiber: 2g   Carbs: 9g   Protein: 25g

---

Falafel
Cook Time: 5 minutes   **Servings: 6**
Ingredients:
- 1 cup chickpeas, cooked
- 1 tablespoon lemon juice
- 2 teaspoons water
- 3 tablespoons tahini
- 4-ounces shallots
- 1 teaspoon garlic powder
- 3 garlic cloves
- 1 teaspoon chili flakes
- 1 teaspoon paprika
- ½ cup parsley, chopped
- 1 tablespoon sesame seeds
- ½ teaspoon coriander
- 1 teaspoon cumin
- ½ teaspoon sea salt
- 1 teaspoon salt

Directions:
Place the chickpeas, coriander, cumin, parsley, salt, chili flakes, paprika, garlic powder, and water into a blender. Blend the mix until it is a smooth mass. Slice garlic cloves and shallot and add to the chickpea mixture. Continue to blend for another minute. Combine the sea salt and sesame seeds in a mixing bowl, and stir.

Make medium-sized balls with chickpea mixture, and coat them with sesame seed mix. Pour olive oil into instant pot and set it to sauté mode. Allow oil to heat up for a few minutes, then toss in the falafel to cook for a 5-minutes. Once they have formed a crust transfer them to a paper towel to remove the excess oil. Combine the tahini, sliced garlic, and lemon juice together and whisk. Drizzle tahini sauce over cooked falafel. Serve warm!

Nutritional Information per serving:
Calories: 296   Fat: 13g   Fiber: 1g   Carbs: 9g   Protein: 26g

---

Chickpea Curry
Cook Time: 11 minutes   **Servings: 6**
Ingredients:
- 2 cans (15-ounce) of chickpeas, rinsed and drained
- 1 packed cup kale, chopped
- 2 tablespoons cilantro leaves, for garnish
- 1 lime juiced
- 1 tablespoon honey
- 1 cup vegetable broth
- 1 cup okra, frozen, sliced
- 1 cup corn, frozen
- 1 (14.5-ounce) can tomatoes, crushed, with juice
- 1 tablespoon curry powder
- 2 cloves garlic, minced
- 1 green bell pepper, diced
- 2 tablespoons olive oil

Directions:

Set your instant pot to the sauté setting, add the oil and heat it. Add onion and stir, cook for 4-minutes. Add the bell pepper and garlic and cook for an additional 2 minutes. Add the curry powder and stir, cooking for another 30 seconds. Add the corn, okra, kale, broth, honey, tomatoes and juice, stir. Select the Manual setting on high with a cook time of 5-minutes. Once the cook time is completed, release the pressure naturally in 10-minutes. Divide into serving dishes, and garnish with cilantro leaves. Serve hot!

Nutritional Information per serving:
Calories: 232   Fat: 10g   Fiber: 1g   Carbs: 23g   Protein: 37g

---

Lentil Sloppy Joe's
Cook Time: 30 minutes   ***Servings: 6***
Ingredients:

- 2 cups green lentils
- 3 cups veggie broth
- 1 red bell pepper, stemmed and chopped
- 1 yellow onion, chopped
- 1 (14-ounce) can of tomatoes, crushed
- 1 tablespoon dark brown sugar
- 1 tablespoon Dijon mustard
- 2 tablespoons soy sauce
- 1 tablespoon olive oil
- Salt and black pepper to taste

Directions:
Set your instant pot to the sauté mode, add the oil and heat it. Add the pepper and onion, cook for 3-minutes or until they have softened. Pour in the broth, then add in soy sauce, mustard, lentils, tomatoes, brown sugar, and pepper. Stir until the sugar has dissolved. Close and seal the pot lid. Select Manual setting on high for a cook time of 27-minutes. When the cook time is completed, release the pressure naturally for 15-minutes. Stir before serving on hamburger buns. Serve hot!

Nutritional Information per serving:
Calories: 208   Fat: 17g   Fiber: 1g   Carbs: 8g   Protein: 27g

---

Lentil and Wild Rice Pilaf
Cook Time: 14 minutes   ***Servings: 6***
Ingredients:

- ¼ cup black or green lentils, soak for 30 minutes before cooking
- ¼ cup black/wild rice, soak for 30 minutes before cooking
- ¼ cup brown rice, soak for 30 minutes before cooking
- 3 cloves garlic, minced
- ½ onion, finely chopped
- 1 stalk celery, finely chopped
- 1 cup mushrooms, sliced
- 2 cups vegetable broth
- ¼ teaspoon red pepper flakes
- Salt and black pepper to taste
- 1 teaspoon fennel seeds
- 1 teaspoon coriander, dried
- 1 tablespoon Italian seasoning
- 1 bay leaf

Directions:

Combine the lentils and rice in a bowl, and allow them to soak for 30-minutes. Drain then rinse well. Set your instant pot to the sauté mode. Sauté veggies in pot for about 5-minutes, add a bit of water to prevent the veggies from burning. Add the rice and lentils, vegetable broth, and spices into pot. Close the lid and set to Manual on high pressure with a cook time of 9-minutes. When the cook time is completed, release the pressure naturally for 10-minutes. Serve dish with fresh or steamed veggies. Serve warm!

Nutritional Information per serving:
Calories: 187   Fat: 11g   Fiber: 1g   Carbs: 7g   Protein: 23g

---

Instant Pot Hummus
Cook Time: 18 minutes **Servings: 6**
Ingredients:

- 1 cup soaked chickpeas
- 6 cups water
- 1 bay leaf
- 4 garlic cloves, crushed
- ¼ cup parsley, chopped
- 2 tablespoons tahini
- Dash of paprika
- ¼ teaspoon cumin
- ¼ teaspoon salt

Directions:
Soak your chickpeas in water overnight. When you are ready to make the hummus, rinse them and place them into instant pot. Pour in 6 cups of water to pot, add garlic cloves, and bay leaf. Seal the lid of pot shut, and set to Manual on high for a cook time of 18-minutes. When the cook time is completed, release the pressure naturally for 10-minutes. When it is safe to do so, once the pressure has come down, then drain the chickpeas, saving 1 cup of cooking liquid. Remove the bay leaf, before pureeing the chickpeas. Add the tahini, lemon juice, cumin, and ½ cup of cooking liquid to start. Keep pureeing, and if the mixture is not creamy enough, add a bit more liquid. Add salt and puree once more when you reach the right creaminess. Serve with a sprinkle of paprika and fresh, chopped parsley as garnish. Serve at room temperature!

Nutritional Information per serving:
Calories: 153   Fat: 4g   Fiber: 2g   Carbs: 8.2g   Protein: 21g

---

Stewed Chickpeas
Cook Time: 27 minutes **Servings: 4**
Ingredients:

- 2 (14-ounce) cans of chickpeas, rinsed and drained
- 1 ½ tablespoon smoked paprika
- 3 small onions, chopped
- ¼ teaspoon allspice
- ½ teaspoon sea salt
- ½ teaspoon cumin
- 1 jar (24-ounces) tomatoes, strained
- 2/3 cup dates, pitted, chopped
- 3 tablespoons water, or as needed

Directions:
Set your instant pot to the sauté mode, add water as needed to prevent sticking. Cook for about 7-minutes, occasionally stirring. Add the tomatoes, dates, chickpeas, and stir until

combined. Cover and lock the pot lid in place and set to Manual on high for a cook time of 20-minutes. When cook time is over, release the pressure using quick-release. Serve over cooked whole-grain, such as millet, quinoa, and brown rice.

Nutritional Information per serving:
Calories: 192   Fat: 16g   Fiber: 1g   Carbs: 6.2g   Protein: 24g

---

Rainbow Beans
Cook Time: 20 minutes   **Servings: 6**
Ingredients:
- 1 cup chicken stock
- 1 cup black beans, cooked
- ½ cup red beans, cooked
- ½ cup green beans, chopped
- ½ cup white beans, cooked
- 1 red sweet pepper, chopped, seeded
- 1 yellow sweet pepper, chopped, seeded
- 1 red onion, chopped
- 3 tablespoons sour cream
- 1 teaspoon turmeric
- 3 tablespoons tomato paste
- Salt as needed

Directions:
Add the water and chicken stock into your instant pot. Add the red, white, and black beans. Add the chopped veggies to instant pot. Sprinkle mixture with turmeric, tomato paste, sour cream, and salt. Mix gently and close the lid. Set to the Stew mode and cook for a 20-minute cook time. When the cooking is completed, transfer to serving bowls. Serve hot!

Nutritional Information per serving:
Calories: 205   Fat: 17g   Fiber: 1g   Carbs: 8.2g   Protein: 27g

---

Northern White Bean Dip
Cook Time: 13 minutes   **Servings: 2**
Ingredients:
- ¾ cup Great Northern white beans, soaked overnight
- Pinch of red pepper flakes
- 1 ½ teaspoons chili powder
- 2 teaspoons cumin, ground
- 3 tablespoons cilantro, minced
- 3 tablespoons lemon juice
- 2 garlic cloves
- 1/3 cup extra virgin olive oil
- Salt and black pepper to taste
- Water as needed

Directions:
Drain the beans before putting them in the instant pot. Cover beans with 1-inch of fresh water, close the pot lid and seal. Select Manual setting on high with a cook time of 13-minutes. When the cook time is completed, release the pressure naturally for 10-minutes. Once the pressure is gone, drain the beans and run under cold water. In a food processor, chop up the garlic. Add the rest of the ingredients (except cilantro) and puree till smooth. Serve with cilantro on top as a garnish. Serve at room temperature!

Nutritional Information per serving:
Calories: 203   Fat: 11g   Fiber: 2g   Carbs: 19g   Protein: 36g

Greek-Style Gigantes Beans with Feta
Cook Time: 25 minutes   **Servings:** 8
Ingredients:
- 3 cups Gigantes white beans, dried
- 8 cups water
- 1 teaspoon oregano, dried
- 1 can (about 28-ounces) crushed tomatoes
- 1 large yellow onion, finely diced
- 1 garlic, clove, peeled
- ¼ cup extra virgin olive oil
- 1 teaspoon salt
- ¼ teaspoon black pepper
- ¼ cup flat-leaf parsley, fresh, chopped, for garnish
- ½ cup feta cheese, crumbled, for garnish or topping

Directions:
Combine the beans, salt, and water in the instant pot. Allow the beans to soak in the water for 12 hours before cooking. Secure the lid in place when you are ready to cook. Select the Bean/Chili setting and set the cook time for 15-minutes at high pressure. When the cook time is completed, release the pressure naturally for 15-minutes. Remove lid and ladle out 1 cup of cooking liquid and set aside. Wearing oven-mitts, lift the inner pot out of instant pot and drain the beans in a colander. Return the now empty pot to the instant pot housing for it. Now, select sauté mode, and heat the ¼ cup olive oil in the pot. Add the garlic, onion, celery and sauté for 15-minutes. Add the drained beans, and reserved cup of cooking liquid, tomatoes, oregano, pepper, and stir well.

Close and lock the lid, and reset the instant pot to Bean/Chili setting and set the cook time for 5-minutes on high. Let the pressure release using quick-release. Ladle the beans into a serving dish and garnish or top with feta cheese, parsley, and remaining olive oil, and serve warm!

Nutritional Information per serving:
Calories: 215   Fat: 18g   Fiber: 2g   Carbs: 7.4g   Protein: 28g

Chili Con Carne
Cook Time: 10 minutes   **Servings:** 6
Ingredients:
- 1 can (28-ounces) ground and peeled tomatoes
- 1 teaspoon oregano, dry
- 1 tablespoon Worcestershire sauce
- 1 tablespoon chili powder
- 1 ½ cups onion, large, diced
- 1 ½ teaspoons cumin, ground
- 1 ½ lbs. ground beef
- 1 can (14-ounce) black beans, rinsed and drained
- 1 can (14-ounce) kidney beans, rinsed and drained
- 3 tablespoons extra virgin olive oil
- 2 tablespoons garlic, minced
- 1-2 jalapenos, stems and seeds removed, finely diced
- Salt and black pepper to taste
- 1 cup sweet red bell pepper, large, diced
- ½ cup water

Directions:

Press the sauté button, allow pot to heat, add in oil. Add the ground beef, and break it up using a wooden spoon, cook for 5-minutes or until beef is browned. Remove excess fat, add the onions, bell pepper, jalapenos, and sauté for 3-minutes. Add the garlic, chili powder, oregano, cumin, salt and pepper, and sauté for 1-minute. Add the beans, water, tomatoes, and Worcestershire sauce and stir to combine. Close and secure the lid. Select Manual setting on high with a cook time of 10-minutes. When the cook time is completed, release the pressure using the quick-release. Serve hot!

Nutritional Information per serving:
Calories: 204   Fat: 22g   Fiber: 2g   Carbs: 17g   Protein: 26g

---

Smokey Sweet Black-Eyed Peas & Greens
Cook Time: 13 minutes   **Servings: 6**
Ingredients:

- 1 ½ teaspoon chili powder
- 2 teaspoons smoked paprika
- 1 ½ cups black-eyed peas, dried and soaked overnight
- 1 cup red pepper, diced
- 1 onion, thinly sliced
- 1 teaspoon oil
- 4 dates, chopped fine
- 1 cup water or vegetable stock
- 1 (15-ounce) can of fire roasted tomatoes with green chilies
- 2 cups greens, chopped, kale or Swiss chard
- Salt to taste

Directions:
Set your instant pot to the sauté mode, add the oil and heat it. Add the onions, and cook for 3-minutes. Add the garlic and peppers and sauté for another 2-minutes. Add the smoked paprika and chili powder along with the peas and dates. Stir to coat them with spices. Add water, stirring to combine. Close and lock lid of pot, select Manual setting on high with a cook time of 3-minutes. When the cook time is completed, release the pressure naturally for 5-minutes. Add the tomatoes and greens and lock the lid, setting for an additional 5-minutes of cook time. Serve warm!

Nutritional Information per serving:
Calories: 207   Fat: 5g   Fiber: 8g   Carbs: 22g   Protein: 29g

---

Tex Mex Pinto Beans
Cook Time: 42 minutes   **Servings: 6**
Ingredients:

- ¼ cup cilantro, chopped
- 1 jalapeno, diced
- 1 onion, chopped
- 1 packet taco seasoning
- ½ cup Salsa Verde
- 1 clove garlic, diced
- 5 cups chicken broth
- 20 ounces package pinto beans with ham

Directions:
Rinse and sort out the dried beans, then place them into your instant pot. Add the broth to the pot. Add onion, garlic, jalapeno, and stir. Add taco seasoning and stir to combine, then close the lid and secure it. Select the Manual setting on high for a cook time of 42-minutes.

When the cook time is completed, release the pressure naturally for about 15-minutes. Drain the excess liquid from the pot. Stir in the Salsa Verde, ham seasoning, and cilantro. Add salt to taste. Serve tacos, over rice, or a side dish. Serve hot!

Nutritional Information per serving:
Calories: 232   Fat: 21g   Fiber: 3g   Carbs: 22g   Protein: 27g

---

Instant Pot Charros
Cook Time: 56 minutes   **Servings: 8**
Ingredients:

- 1 lb. pinto beans dried, rinsed and picked over
- ½ lb. double smoked bacon
- ½ lb. Mexican Chorizo raw, Mexican chorizo sausage, not the dried Spanish chorizo
- 1 large onion, chopped
- 1 large jalapeno, seeded and finely chopped
- 4 cloves garlic
- 1 can of tomatoes and chilies
- 3 cups chicken stock
- 2 cups Mexican beer
- 2 chipotle chilies canned in adobo, minced
- 1 teaspoon salt
- 2 bay leaves
- 1 tablespoon Epazote, crushed
- 1 tablespoon Mexican oregano
- 2 tablespoons cumin
- 1 tablespoon olive oil
- 1 cup cilantro, fresh, chopped, for garnish

Directions:
Set your instant pot to the sauté mode, add the oil and heat it up. Add the bacon and fry until it starts to brown for about 5-minutes. Remove the chorizo meat from the casing and add it to pot to brown. Cook for another 4-minutes or until meat is cooked.
Add the onion, add cook for another 5-minutes. Add the jalapenos, cumin, garlic, oregano, Epazote and cook for one more minute. Now add in the pinto beans, bay leaves, chipotle chilies, beer, salt, chicken stock, and give it a nice stir. Close the lid and set to cook for 45-minutes on Manual high with a cook time of 45-minutes. When the cook time is completed, release the pressure naturally for 15-minutes. Remove the lid and stir the beans, and set to sauté mode, cooking for an additional 5-minutes. Serve hot! Top with cilantro for garnish.

Nutritional Information per serving:
Calories: 243   Fat: 20g   Fiber: 2g   Carbs: 21g   Protein: 31g

---

Three Bean Salad
Cook Time: 15 minutes   **Servings: 4**
Ingredients:

- 1 cup chickpeas/garbanzo beans, soaked or quick-soaked
- 1 cup Borlotti or cranberry beans, soaked or quick-soaked
- 1 ½ cups of green beans, fresh or frozen
- 1 bay leaf
- 1 clove of garlic, lightly crushed

For the dressing:

- 2 celery stalks, chopped finely
- ½ red onion, chopped finely
- 4 tablespoon olive oil
- 1 teaspoon Truvia
- 5 tablespoon apple cider vinegar
- 1 bunch parsley, finely chopped
- Salt and pepper to taste

Directions:
Wrap the green beans inside some aluminum foil. Add 4 cups of fresh water to your instant pot, then add the soaked or rinsed chickpeas, garlic clove, and bay leaf. Add the steamer basket with the soaked Borlotti beans. Finally, add the packet of tin foil wrapped green beans. Use a second trivet to keep your packet suspended above the Borlotti. Close and lock the pot lid, and set to Manual on high for a cook time of 15-minutes.

When the cook time is completed, release the pressure naturally for 10-minutes. While the beans are cooking prepare dressing. Slice the onion nice and fine, add to a bowl with vinegar and Truvia, mix and set aside. Remove and open the packet of green beans. Pour the beans from the steamer basket and into a strainer. Rinse beans under cold water. Slice the green beans and place in with other beans and mix well. In a serving bowl add the beans along with dressing and mix well. Add salt and pepper to taste. Serve chilled!

Nutritional Information per serving:
Calories: 198   Fat: 18g   Fiber: 3g   Carbs: 19g   Protein: 29g

---

Beans Stew
Cook Time: 67 minutes   **Servings: 8**

Ingredients:
- 1 lb. red beans, dry—water as needed
- 2 carrots, chopped
- 2 tablespoons vegetable oils
- ¼ cup cilantro leaves, chopped
- 1 small onion, diced
- 2 green onions, chopped
- 1 tomato, chopped
- Salt and black pepper to taste
- 2 carrots, chopped
- Water as needed

Directions:
Add the beans to your instant pot and set to Manual on high for a cook time of 35-minutes. When the cook time is completed, release the pressure naturally for 10-minutes. Add carrots, and salt and pepper to taste, cover instant pot again, setting for a cook time of 30-additional minutes. Meanwhile heat a pan with vegetable oil over medium high heat, add onion, stir for 2-minutes. Add tomatoes, green onions, some salt and pepper and stir again, cook for an additional 3-minutes, then remove from heat. Release the pressure naturally for 10-minutes. Divide among serving plates, and garnish with fresh, chopped cilantro. Serve warm!

Nutritional Information per serving:
Calories: 211   Fat: 23g   Fiber: 1g   Carbs: 26g   Protein: 29g

Not Re-Fried Beans
Cook Time: 13 minutes
Servings: 8
Ingredients:
- 2 cups Borlotti beans, dried, soaked
- 2 cups water
- ½ teaspoon cumin
- ¼ teaspoon chipotle powder
- 1 bunch cilantro or parsley, leaves and stems, chopped, divided
- 1 onion, chopped
- 1 tablespoon vegetable oil
- 1 teaspoon salt

Directions:
Set your instant pot to the saute mode, add the oil and heat. Add the onion and cook for 3-minutes. Add beans and water. Close and lock the lid to pot, and set on Manual on high with a cook time of 10-minutes. When the cook time is completed, release the pressure naturally for 10-minutes. Remove a heaping spoonful of beans from pot and set aside (to use as garnish). Sprinkle the rest of the beans inside pot with salt and mash with potato masher for desired consistency. Serve with sprinkled whole beans, parsley, and a dollop of sour cream as garnish. Serve warm!

Nutritional Information per serving:
Calories: 213   Fat: 20g   Fiber: 2g   Carbs: 14g   Protein: 31g

Baked Beans
Cook Time: 23 minutes
Servings: 8
Ingredients:
- 1 lb. dried navy beans, soaked overnight for at least 16 hours
- 1 teaspoon apple cider vinegar
- 2 teaspoons Dijon mustard
- 2 bay leaves
- ¼ teaspoon fine table salt
- 1 tablespoon light soy sauce
- ¼ cup maple syrup
- ¼ cup blackstrap molasses
- 1 ¾ cup cold water
- 2 cloves garlic, roughly chopped
- 1 small onion, roughly diced
- 6 strips thick-cut bacon, roughly diced
- 6 cups cold water

Directions:
Allow the navy beans to soak overnight in a container filled with 6 cups of water with 1 ½ tablespoons of fine table salt. After they have soaked for the night drain the water out of the navy beans using a mesh strainer. Rinse the beans with cold water, drain well. The soaked beans should double in weight. Place the chopped bacon into your instant pot and set it to the sauté mode, stir occasionally, cooking for 3-minutes. Add in the diced onion, pepper, and sauté for another additional minute. Add in the chopped garlic cloves and sauté for 30 seconds.

Combine ¼ cup blackstrap molasses, ¼ cup maple syrup, 1 tablespoon light soy sauce, and 1 ¾ cup cold water in a 1-liter glass measuring cup, and mix well. Pour ½ cup of molasses mixture into your instant pot. Mix well.

Add ¼ teaspoon fine table salt, 2 bay leaves, soaked navy beans, and the remaining molasses mixture into instant pot. Mix well. Close the lid and set to Manual on high with a cook time of 20-minutes. When the cook time is completed, release the pressure naturally for 20-minutes. Add 2 teaspoons of Dijon mustard, and 1 teaspoon apple cider vinegar into the cooked baked beans. Mix well. Set your instant pot to the sauté mode and heat the pot and stir baked beans until they get the desired consistency. Serve this as a side dish at family picnics, or potlucks, or dinner. Serve hot!

Nutritional Information per serving:
Calories: 206   Fat: 23g   Fiber: 3g   Carbs: 19g   Protein: 33g

---

Stewed Tomatoes & Green Beans
Cook Time: 10 minutes   **Servings: 10**
Ingredients:
- 1 lb. green beans
- 2 cups tomatoes, fresh, chopped
- 1 crushed garlic clove
- 1 teaspoon olive oil
- ½ cup water
- Salt to taste

Directions:
Set your instant pot to the sauté mode, add the oil and heat it. Add the garlic, and once it becomes fragrant add tomatoes, and ½ cup water. Fill the steamer basket with green beans and sprinkle salt and lower into instant pot. Close and seal the lid to pot and set to Manual on high for a cook time of 5-minutes. When the cook time is completed, release the pressure naturally for 10-minutes. Remove steamer basket from pot and pour the beans into the tomato sauce and stir. Serve warm!

Nutritional Information per serving:
Calories: 198   Fat: 6g   Fiber: 2g   Carbs: 15g   Protein: 23g

Chapter 10. Vegetable Instant Pot Recipes

Sweet Potato, Red Lentil, Hemp Burgers
Cook Time: 16 minutes   **Servings:** 10
Ingredients:

- 1 cup onion, minced
- 1 cup cremini mushrooms, minced
- 2 ¼ cups vegetable stock
- 2 teaspoons ginger, fresh, grated
- 1 ½ sweet potatoes, peeled, cut into large pieces
- 1 cup red lentils, rinsed and picked over
- ¼ cup of hemp seeds
- 4 tablespoons of brown rice flour
- ¼ cup flat leaf parsley, fresh, chopped finely
- 1 cup quick oats
- ¼ cup cilantro, chopped finely
- 1 tablespoon curry powder

Directions:
Set your instant pot on the sauté mode, add in the mushrooms, ginger, and onion, dry sauté for 3-minutes. Add in the sweet potatoes, lentils and vegetable stock. Close and secure the lid, set to Manual on high for a cook time of 6-minutes. When the cook time is completed, release the pressure naturally for 10-minutes. Transfer the lentil mixture to a bowl, and allow to stand for 15-minutes at room temperature. Heat your oven to 375° Fahrenheit. Line a large baking sheet with parchment paper, and lightly coat it with cooking spray. Mash the lentil mixture with a potato masher, when cool. Stir in the cilantro, parsley and hemp seeds, as well as curry powder, then stir in oats.
Add in the brown rice flour, and form the mixture into 10 patties using wet hands and place each patty onto the already prepared baking sheet. Bake for 10-minutes; flip and bake until they are firm and brown, cook for an additional 10-minutes. Allow to cool for a couple of minutes. Serve immediately, or freeze, or refrigerate for later use. Serve warm.

Nutritional Information per serving:
Calories: 263   Fat: 1.3g   Carbs: 53.6g   Protein: 9.8g

Creamy Kidney Beans & Lentils
Cook Time: 45 minutes   **Servings:** 6
Ingredients:

- 3 cups kidney beans, cooked
- 6 garlic cloves, minced
- 1 teaspoon cardamom, ground
- 1 cup of whole black lentils, dry
- 2 tablespoons ginger, grated
- 1 ½ teaspoons chili powder
- 3 teaspoons cumin, ground
- ¼ teaspoon nutmeg, ground
- 1 teaspoon turmeric, ground
- 5 cups of water
- ¼ teaspoon mustard, ground

Before serving:

- 2 teaspoons ginger, grated
- ½ cup cashew creamer
- Cilantro, fresh, chopped for garnish
- 1 teaspoon garam masala

- Salt to taste

Directions:
Add all the ingredients to your instant pot, and set on Manual on high for a cook time of 45-minutes. When the cook time has completed, release the pressure naturally for 15-minutes. Once the cooking is completed stir in the serving ingredients and serve hot.

Nutritional Information per serving:
Calories: 250   Fat: 1.4g   Carbs: 45.6g   Protein: 16.5g

Sweet Potato, Lentil & Coconut Curry
Cook Time: 13 minutes   Servings: 4
Ingredients:

- 3 ½ cups vegetable broth
- 1 carrot, large, sliced lengthwise and chopped
- 1 cup red or green lentils, dried
- 1 ½ tablespoons coconut oil
- 1 cup onion, diced
- 1 tablespoon curry powder
- ½ teaspoon turmeric, ground
- ½ cup coconut milk
- Fresh ground black pepper to taste
- 1 teaspoon ginger powder
- 1 sweet potato, medium, cubed into 1-inch cubes
- Sea salt to taste

Directions:
Set your instant pot to sauté mode, and heat the oil. Sauté the onion for 3-minutes. Add in the carrot, potato, lentils and seasonings to taste; stir several times to combine. Add the broth and close and secure the lid. Set to Manual on high for a cook time of 10-minutes. When the cook time is completed, release the pressure naturally for 10-minutes. Stir in the coconut milk and season with salt and pepper to taste. Serve warm.

Nutritional Information per serving:
Calories: 234   Fat: 11.8g   Carbs: 27.2g   Protein: 7.2g

Millet & Lentils with Vegetables & Mushrooms
Cook Time: 15 minutes   Servings: 4
Ingredients:

- ½ cup French green lentils, rinsed and picked over
- 1 cup sugar snap peas, sliced
- 2 garlic cloves, minced
- 1 cup millet, rinsed
- 2 ¼ cups vegetable stock
- 1 cup leek, sliced
- ½ cup Bok Choy, sliced thinly
- Drizzle of lemon juice, fresh
- ¼ cup herbs, fresh, chopped such as parsley mixed with chives and garlic
- ½ cup oyster mushrooms, sliced thinly
- 1 cup asparagus, cut into 1-inch pieces
- Sesame salt for garnish

Directions:
Set your instant pot to the sauté mode, then add the leek, mushrooms, and garlic, dry sauté for 3-minutes. Add the lentils and millet; toast for a minute and then add in the vegetable stock. Close and secure the lid on the pot, and select the Manual setting on high with a cook

time of 10-minutes. Once the cook time is completed, release the pressure naturally for 10-minutes. Add in the asparagus, Bok Choy, and peas. Place the lid back on pot and set on Manual for an additional 5-minutes cook time. Stir and add the herbs, and then transfer to a large bowl. Add the lemon juice and sprinkle sesame salt over before serving. Serve warm.

Nutritional Information per serving:
Calories: 146   Fat: 1g   Carbs: 28g   Protein: 7.9g

Basmati Rice
Cook Time: 6 minutes   ***Servings: 6***
Ingredients:
- 1 red bell pepper, diced
- 2 cups long-grain or basmati rice
- 1 medium onion, chopped
- 1 carrot, grated
- 1 tablespoon olive oil
- ½ cup peas, fresh or frozen
- 1 teaspoon salt
- Water as needed
- 1 teaspoon turmeric, powder

Directions:
Set your instant pot to the sauté mode, add the olive oil and heat it. Add the onion and cook for 3-minutes. Add carrot, bell pepper in a 1 litre liquid measuring cup; lightly pat down into an even layer. Pour water into the veggie container until you reach the 750ml mark then set aside. Add rice, peas, turmeric and salt to your instant pot; add the ingredients from measuring cup and give mix a good stir. Close and secure the lid of pot, and set on Manual on high for a cook time of 3-minutes. When the cook time is completed, release the pressure naturally for 10-minutes. Use a large fork to fluff the rice and serve warm.

Vegan Butter Chickpeas
Cook Time: 6 minutes   ***Servings: 6***
Ingredients:
- 1 can of garbanzo beans, drained
- 1 cup of coconut milk
- 1 ½ cups vegetable broth
- 1 packet of extra firm tofu
- 1 teaspoon of chili powder
- 1 cup of rice
- 1 tablespoon curry powder
- 1 tablespoon of garam masala
- ½ cup tomatoes, crushed
- Pepper and salt to taste

Directions:
Cube the tofu and add to instant pot along with crushed tomatoes, garbanzo beans, coconut milk, and spices. Close and secure the lid and set to Manual on high with a cook time of 2-minutes. Once the cooking is completed, release the pressure naturally for 10-minutes. Add the veggie broth and rice to instant pot and close lid, set to Manual on high with a cook time of 4-minutes. When the cook time is completed, release the pressure naturally for 10-minutes. Serve hot.

Potatoes & Peas
Cook Time: 12 minutes **Servings: 4**
Ingredients:
- 1 large tomato
- ½ teaspoon cumin, ground
- 1 teaspoon coriander, ground
- ½ teaspoon garam masala
- 1-inch of ginger, chopped
- 7 garlic cloves
- 1 teaspoon mustard seeds
- ½ teaspoon of red chili powder
- 1 red onion, small, chopped
- 3 medium potatoes, chopped into ½-inch pieces
- ½ teaspoon turmeric
- ¼ cup peas, fresh
- 2 teaspoons coconut oil
- ¾ teaspoon salt
- 1 cup water
- 1 cup cilantro, fresh, chopped for garnish

Directions:
Set your instant pot to the sauté mode, and heat the coconut oil. Add cumin and mustard seeds, and cook for 2-minutes. Add in onion, mix well and cook for an additional 3-minutes. Blend the ginger, tomato and garlic until you get a coarse puree. Add the tomato puree and spices to your instant pot.
Cook for 5-minutes or until puree thickens. Add the potatoes, water and salt, set to Manual setting with a cook time of 4-minutes. When the cook time completes, release the pressure naturally for 10-minutes. Add in the spinach and peas, mix well. Sauté mix for 2-minutes. Garnish with fresh, chopped cilantro and serve warm.

Nutritional Information per serving:
Calories: 209 Fat: 3.2g Carbs: 40.6g Protein: 6.8g

Spicy Veggie Mix
Cook Time: 17 minutes **Servings: 2**
Ingredients:
- 2 cups cauliflower florets
- 1 ½ teaspoons mustard, ground
- ¼ teaspoon turmeric
- ¼ cup water
- 1 cup sweet potato, chopped
- 1 cup green beans, chopped
- ½ cup green peas
- 1/8 teaspoon asafetida
- 1 teaspoon olive oil
- ½ teaspoon sugar
- 1 cup potato, chopped
- Salt to taste
- 1 teaspoon of Panch Phoron

Directions:
Add the ground mustard with water and turmeric, potato, green beans, cauliflower florets and salt into your instant pot. Set to Manual on high with a cook time of 5-minutes. When the cook time is completed, release the pressure naturally for 10-minutes. In a small skill over medium heat add the oil along with Panch pharon, and spices and cook for 2-minutes. Add chilies and asafetida to pan and cook for an additional 2-minutes. Add mixture to instant pot with peas and some salt and sauté for 2-minutes. Serve hot.

Nutritional Information per serving:
Calories: 106   Fat: 3.3g   Carbs: 17.3g   Protein: 4.8g

Vegetable Masala Mix
Cook Time: 10 minutes   **Servings: 4**
Ingredients:

- 3 cups veggies, chopped such as peppers, carrots and cauliflower, Green beans, potatoes, zucchini, cabbage etc.
- ½ teaspoon cayenne
- 3 garlic cloves, minced
- ½ teaspoon each of mustard, cumin, coriander, turmeric
- 1/3 cup green peas
- Cilantro, fresh, chopped, and lemon for garnish
- Black pepper and salt to taste
- 1 teaspoon oil
- ½ teaspoon cinnamon

Directions:
Mix all the spices in a mixing bowl, and set aside. Set your instant pot to the sauté mode, and heat oil and add in the garlic, cooking it for 2-minutes. Add in the spice mix and cook for an additional minute. Add the veggies, water and salt into instant pot and stir. Close the lid to pot and select the Manual setting with a cook time of 2-minutes. Release the pressure using quick-release. Add in the peas to the pot then close the lid and set to Manual on a cook time for 5-minutes. Garnish with fresh, chopped cilantro and lemon. Serve warm.

Nutritional Information per serving:
Calories: 278   Fat: 3.3g   Carbs: 56.2g   Protein: 12.4g

Masala Eggplant
Cook Time: 10 minutes   **Servings: 3**
Ingredients:

- 2 tablespoons cashews
- ½ teaspoon mustard seeds
- ½ teaspoon turmeric
- 1 hot green Chile, chopped
- ½ teaspoon cardamom, ground
- 1 ½ ginger, chopped
- 2 tablespoons coconut shreds
- 2 garlic cloves, chopped
- ½ teaspoon cumin seeds
- 1 tablespoon coriander seeds
- 3 tablespoons chickpea flour
- Water as needed
- ½ teaspoon salt
- 1 teaspoon lime juice
- ½ teaspoon raw sugar
- ½ teaspoon cayenne

For Curry:

- 6 baby eggplants
- 1 cup water
- Fresh cilantro, garam masala, and coconut for garnish

Directions:
Set your instant pot to the sauté mode, add the mustard, coriander and cumin seeds and brown for 2-minutes. Add the chickpea flour and mix for a minute. Add in nuts and coconut and mix well. Allow to cool and transfer to a food processor and process to coarsely grind.

Add in the garlic, Chile, lime, ginger and remaining ground spices; pulse until you get a coarse mixture, add a teaspoon of water. Make cross cuts on the eggplants and fill the cross cuts with the stuffing. Place the eggplants into your instant pot. Add a cup of water and some salt, along with a cup of cooked beans. Set to Manual setting for 5-minutes cook time. When the cook time is completed, release the pressure naturally for 10-minutes. Garnish with fresh, chopped cilantro, coconut, garam masala, and serve with rice or flatbread. Serve warm.

Nutritional Information per serving:
Calories: 783   Fat: 21.6g   Carbs: 144.7g   Protein: 20.9g

Mushroom Matar Masala
Cook Time: 20 minutes   **Servings: 2**
Ingredients:

- ½ teaspoon paprika
- 1 cup spinach, fresh, chopped
- ¾ cup peas
- 1-inch of ginger
- 1/3 cup cashews, raw and soaked for 15-minutes
- 5 garlic cloves
- ½ teaspoon garam masala
- 1 green chile, remove seeds
- 2 large tomatoes
- ½ large onion, chopped
- 8-ounces of white mushrooms, sliced
- 1 teaspoon fenugreek leaves, dried
- ¼ teaspoon sugar
- Cayenne to taste
- ½ teaspoon salt
- 1 teaspoon coconut oil
- Cilantro, fresh, chopped for garnish

Directions:
Puree the garlic with onion, chile, ginger and a few tablespoons of water in a blender on high speed. Set your instant pot to the sauté mode, and heat the oil. Add the pureed mixture to instant pot and heat for 3-minutes, stirring occasionally.

In the meantime, blend the tomatoes and cashews until smooth. Add this puree with the garam masala, fenugreek, and paprika into the instant pot. Saute for 7-minutes, stirring occasionally. Add the peas, mushrooms, other veggies, sugar, salt and ½ cup of water and mix well. Cover and cook on Manual for a cook time of 10-minutes. Garnish with fresh chopped cilantro and serve with rice or flat bread. Serve warm.

Nutritional Information per serving:
Calories: 334   Fat: 14.6g   Carbs: 43.7g   Protein: 15.2g

Curried Potato Eggplant
Cook Time: 8 minutes   **Servings: 2**
Ingredients:

- 1 eggplant, medium, thinly chopped
- 6 curry leaves, chopped
- 4 garlic cloves, minced
- 1 tomato, large, crushed, chopped finely
- 1 teaspoon coriander powder
- ¾ cup water
- Garam masala or pure red chili powder to taste
- 1 teaspoon coconut oil

- Cilantro, fresh, chopped for garnish
- ¾ teaspoon salt
- 1 potato, large, cubed into small pieces
- ½ teaspoon mustard seeds, cumin and turmeric seeds
- 1 hot green chile, chopped finely
- ½ an inch of ginger, minced

Directions:
Set your instant pot to the sauté mode, add the oil and heat it. Add the mustard and cumin seeds and cook for a minute. Add in the curry leaves, ginger, garlic and chili. Add in turmeric, coriander, tomatoes and mix well, cooking for an additional 2-minutes. Now add everything into your instant pot and close and secure the lid. Select the Manual setting on high for a cook time of 5-minutes. Once the cook time is completed, release the pressure naturally for 10-minutes. Give everything a good stir. Divide into serving bowls, garnish with fresh chopped cilantro, and serve hot.

Nutritional Information per serving:
Calories: 394   Fat: 22.6g   Carbs: 28.8g   Protein: 29.2g

Coconut Tofu Curry
Cook Time: 4 minutes   *Servings:* 4
Ingredients:
- 1 ½ teaspoons salt
- 1 cup onion, chunks
- 2 cups green bell pepper, chunks
- 1 tablespoon curry powder
- 10-ounces coconut milk, light, canned
- 2 tablespoons peanut butter, creamy
- 1 tablespoon garam masala
- 8-ounces tomato paste
- 2 teaspoons garlic cloves, minced
- 1 cup tofu, firm, diced

Directions:
Add everything to a food processor, except the tofu. Put the tofu inside your instant pot and pour sauce from food processor on top of tofu pieces. Close and secure the pot lid, and set to Manual with a cook time of 4-minutes. Once the cook time has completed, release the pressure using the quick-release. Serve over a bed of rice. Serve hot.

Nutritional Information per serving:
Calories: 259   Fat: 13.8g   Carbs: 27.5g   Protein: 15.2g

Tomato Stewed Green Bean
Cook Time: 10 minutes   *Servings:* 4
Ingredients:
- 1 teaspoon extra virgin olive oil
- 2 pinches of salt
- 1 tablespoon olive oil
- 2 cups tomatoes, fresh, chopped
- 1 sprig basil, leaves removed
- 1 clove garlic, crushed
- 1 lb. green beans, fresh or frozen, remove ends

Directions:
Set your instant pot to the sauté mode, add tablespoon olive oil and heat it. Add the crushed garlic clove and cook for 2-minutes. Add in tomatoes and swirl everything to mix. Add steamer basket filled with green beans. Sprinkle some salt on the beans. Close and lock lid

to pot, and set to Manual with a cook time of 5-minutes. When the cook time is completed, release the pressure using the quick-release. Remove the steamer basket and add the beans in with the tomato sauce at bottom of instant pot. Set on sauté mode for 5-minutes, stirring often. Add bean mix to a large serving bowl, and top with fresh basil leaves and 1 teaspoon of extra-virgin olive oil. Serve warm.

Nutritional Information per serving:
Calories: 95   Fat: 5g   Carbs: 12.4g   Protein: 2.9g

Sesame Tofu
Cooking Time: 8 minutes   **Servings: 4**
Ingredients:
- 1 cup sweet potato, peeled, diced
- 2 teaspoons sesame oil, toasted
- 2 tablespoons sesame seeds
- 1 carrot, peeled, cut diagonally into ½-inch pieces
- 1/3 cup vegetable stock
- 3 garlic cloves, minced
- 2 cups snow peas
- 1 lb. tofu, extra firm, cut into 1-inch cubes
- 2 tablespoons of sweet & spicy red pepper sauce
- 2 tablespoons of tamari
- 2 tablespoons tahini
- 2 cups yellow onion, sliced
- 2 tablespoons scallion, chopped
- 1 tablespoon rice vinegar

Directions:
Set your instant pot to the sauté mode, and add sesame oil and heat it. Add in onion, sweet potato, carrot and sauté for 2-minutes. Add the garlic and tablespoon of sesame seeds, and sauté for an additional 2-minutes. Add in the tofu, tamari, stock, and vinegar. Close and secure the lid of pot, and set to Manual on high with a cook time of 3-minutes. When the cook time is completed, release the pressure using quick-release. Add in the peas and close the lid again, and cook for another 3-minutes, then use the quick-release again. Stir in the tahini and pepper sauce. Use the leftover sesame seeds as a garnish along with green onions chopped. Serve warm.

Nutritional Information per serving:
Calories: 283   Fat: 13.6g   Carbs: 27.3g   Protein: 16.1g

Lentil & Spinach Dal
Cooking Time: 13 minutes   **Servings: 6**
Ingredients:
- 1 red onion, large, chopped
- 3 garlic cloves, minced
- 1 teaspoon coriander, ground
- 4 cups spinach, fresh, chopped
- 1 teaspoon turmeric, ground
- ¼ cup cilantro, fresh, chopped
- 2 teaspoons vegan butter
- 1 teaspoon cumin, ground
- 1 tomato, large, cut into wedges
- 3 cups water
- 1 ½ cups yellow split peas
- ½ teaspoon salt
- ¼ teaspoon cayenne pepper, dried
- 2 tablespoons of olive oil

To Serve:
- Fresh cilantro, chopped
- Plain yogurt
- Cooked naan or brown rice

Directions:
Set your instant pot to the sauté mode, add oil and heat it. Add onions and cook for 2-minutes. Add garlic and stir well. Turn off the heat then add in the cumin, coriander, cayenned, turmeric, and mix until well combined. Add the lentils, tomato wedges, salt and water into instant pot and stir. Close and secure the lid, and set to Manual on a cook time of 10-minutes. When the cook time is completed, release the pressure using the quick-release. Remove and discard the tomato skins, and whisk the lentils to blend. Add in the spinach, cilantro, and vegan butter, stir to combine. Top it with plain yogurt and fresh cilantro, serve with naan or brown rice. Serve hot.

Nutritional Information per serving:
Calories: 210   Fat: 2.7g   Carbs: 35.2g   Protein: 13.5g

Spinach Chana Masala
Cook Time: 18 minutes   **Servings: 6**

Ingredients:
- 1 green chili, chopped
- ½ teaspoon turmeric
- 1 tablespoon Chana masala/cholay
- 1 tablespoon garlic, grated
- 2 cups tomato puree, fresh
- ½ tablespoon ginger, grated
- 1 bay leaf
- 3 tablespoons olive oil
- 1 cup onions, chopped
- 1 cup Chana/cholay/chickpeas, raw, soaked for overnight
- 2 teaspoons chili powder
- 1 teaspoon coriander powder
- 2 cups baby spinach, fresh, chopped
- Lemon, fresh
- Handful of cilantro, fresh, chopped
- Salt to taste

Directions:
Clean the chickpeas under cold running water, the next morning drain excess water from the soaked chickpeas. Set your instant pot to the sauté mode, add oil and heat it. Add onions and cook for 2-minutes. Add green chili, bay leaf, ginger, and garlic paste and cook for an additional 2-minutes.
Add in the Chana masala, turmeric, chili powder, coriander powder along with a tablespoon of water. Continue to sauté for a few more seconds. Add in the roasted chickpea flour and sauté for a few more seconds. Now add in the drained chickpeas, tomato puree, and water, mix well. Close and lock the lid to pot, and set to Manual for a cook time of 15-minutes. Once the cook time is completed, release the pressure naturally for 10-minutes. Set pot to sauté mode again and add in the spinach and salt and cook for another 3-minutes, stir. Add in some lemon juice, and chopped coriander. Serve warm, with chapatti, or over quinoa/rice.

Nutritional Information per serving:
Calories: 362   Fat: 14.9g   Carbs: 46.4g   Protein: 14.3g

Lentil Bolognese
Cook Time: 15 minutes   **Servings:** 4
Ingredients:
- 1 cup of Beluga black lentils, washed
- 3 carrots, medium, diced
- 4 garlic cloves, minced
- 1 can of fire roasted tomatoes, chopped
- Red pepper flakes to taste
- 2 tablespoons Italian seasoning, dry
- 1 can tomato paste
- Pepper and salt to taste
- 4 cups water
- Balsamic vinegar to taste
- 1 yellow onion, diced

Directions:
Add everything into your instant pot, except the vinegar, salt and pepper. Stir well to mix ingredients. Close the lid of pot, and set to Manual on high with a cook time of 15-minutes. When the cook time is completed, release pressure with quick-release. Add drizzle of balsamic and stir. Serve hot over pasta.

Nutritional Information per serving:
Calories: 137 Fat: 1.1g Carbs: 28g Protein: 7.8g

Coconut Quinoa Curry
Cook Time: 45 minutes   **Servings:** 6
Ingredients:
- 1 tablespoon turmeric, ground
- ¼ cup quinoa
- 1 can (15-ounce) of organic chickpeas, drained, rinsed
- 3 cups sweet potato, peeled, chopped
- 1 cup white onion, diced
- 2 cups broccoli crowns, cut into florets
- 1 can (28-ounce) tomatoes, diced
- 2 cans coconut milk (14.5 ounce each)
- 1 tablespoon garlic cloves, minced
- 2 teaspoons tamari sauce, wheat free
- 1 tablespoon ginger, freshly grated
- 1 teaspoon chili flakes
- 1 teaspoon tamari

Directions:
Add 1 cup of water into your instant pot, and add all ingredients into pot. Stir well. Close and lock the pot lid, and set to Manual for a cook time of 45-minutes. When the cook time is completed, release the pressure naturally for 15-minutes. Serve hot.

Nutritional Information per serving:
Calories: 412 Fat: 10.3g Carbs: 72.1g Protein: 13.7g

Garlic Mashed Potatoes
Cook Time: 4 minutes   **Servings:** 4
Ingredients:
- ¼ cup parsley, fresh, chopped
- Salt to taste
- 6 garlic cloves, peeled and cut in half
- ½ cup non-dairy milk
- 4 Russet potatoes, cut into chunks
- 1 cup vegetable broth

Directions:
Add the potato chunks, broth, and garlic into your instant pot. Close and secure the lid, and set to Manual with a cook time of 4-minutes on high. When the cook time is completed, release the pressure using quick-release. Mash the potatoes, add soy milk. Add the parsley and salt to taste. Serve hot.

Nutritional Information per serving:
Calories: 146   Fat: 1g   Carbs: 32.4g   Protein: 5.1g

Marinara Sauce
Cook Time: 12 minutes   **Servings: 4**
Ingredients:
- 1 ½ cups of water
- 2 sweet potatoes, large, diced
- 2 cans (28-ounce) tomatoes, crushed
- ½ cup red lentils, remove shriveled lentils
- 3 garlic cloves, minced
- Salt to taste

Directions:
Set your instant pot to sauté mode and cook the garlic, sweet potatoes, lentils and salt for 2-minutes. Add crushed tomatoes and stir well. Set to Manual on high with a cook time of 12-minutes. When the cook time is completed, release the pressure naturally for 15-minutes. Stir and puree using an immersion blender. Serve warm.

Nutritional Information per serving:
Calories: 94   Fat: 0.2g   Carbs: 20.1g   Protein: 3.5g

Cauliflower Rice
Cook Time: 1 minute   **Servings: 4**
Ingredients:
- 1 head of cauliflower, medium, washed and trim leaves, chopped
- ½ teaspoon parsley, dried
- ¼ teaspoon salt
- 2 tablespoons olive oil

Optional Seasonings:
- ¼ teaspoon cumin
- ¼ teaspoon cilantro, fresh, chopped
- ¼ teaspoon turmeric
- Lime juice or lime wedges, fresh
- ¼ teaspoon paprika

Directions:
Place the cauliflower pieces into the steamer and then insert it into your instant pot. Add a cup of water in the steamer basket. Close and secure the pot lid, and set it on Manual on high with a cook time of 1-minute. When the cook time is completed, release the pressure using quick-release. Transfer the cauliflower to a plate. Remove the water from instant pot, and set to sauté mode. Add oil into instant pot, add in the cauliflower and mash with potato masher to break pieces up. Add lime juice and cilantro and stir. Serve warm.

Delicious Dumplings
Cook Time: 9 minutes **Servings: 4**
Ingredients:
- 1 teaspoon ginger, fresh, grated
- ½ cup carrot, shredded
- 1 cup white mushrooms, minced
- 1 ½ cups cabbage, minced
- 1 tablespoon oil
- 2 tablespoons soy sauce
- 1 teaspoon sesame oil
- 12 dumpling wrappers
- 1 tablespoon rice wine vinegar

Directions:
In a large pan over medium heat sauté the minced mushrooms, then add in the carrot, cabbage, vinegar, and soy sauce and cook until mixture becomes dry. Add in sesame oil and ginger in instant pot. Lightly coat vegetable steamer with oil then place it in instant pot. Set a small bowl of water on cutting board. On the cutting board arrange a wrapper using your fingertip; spread water just about the edge. Add a tablespoon of filling to center and fold wrapper in half and match the edges. Press edges together. Add 1 ½ cups of water and the trivet to your instant pot, then place the steamer on top of it. Set to Manual setting for a cook time of 6-minutes. When cook time is completed, release the pressure using quick-release. Serve warm.

Nutritional Information per serving:
Calories: 299 Fat: 10.1g Carbs: 44.9g Protein: 8.4g

Sweet Potato Pie
Cook Time: 13 minutes **Servings: 4**
Ingredients:
- 1 cup tomatoes, fresh, diced
- ½ cup carrot, diced
- 1 cup onion, diced
- ½ cup sweet potato, peeled, diced
- 1 cup French green lentils, rinsed and picked over
- 1/3 cup celery, diced
- 1 garlic clove, minced
- ¼ teaspoon parsley, dried
- ½ teaspoon rosemary, fresh, chopped
- 1 bay leaf
- 1 ¾ cups vegetable stock
- 1 teaspoon thyme, dried
- 1 cup celery, diced
- 2 tablespoons browned rice flower
- 1 tablespoon tomato paste
- 2 teaspoons of tamari
- 1 tablespoon Worcestershire sauce

Directions:
Set your instant pot to sauté mode, add in onion, celery, carrot and cook for 2-minutes. Add in the lentils, potatoes, bay leaf, thyme, stock and rosemary. Secure the lid closed on pot and set to Manual on high for a cook time of 10-minutes. When the cook time is completed, release the pressure with quick-release.
Add in a tablespoon of browned flour, along with tamari, Worcestershire sauce, tomato paste and tomatoes, and stir. Close the lid again and let it cook on sauté mode for 3-minutes and use the quick-release again. Transfer to a large casserole dish; discard the bay leaf. Top

the cooked pie with the mashed potatoes. Run under broiler for a few minutes to brown potatoes. Serve hot.
Nutritional Information per serving:
Calories: 163   Fat: 0.7g   Carbs: 33.4g   Protein: 7.5g

Tasty Tofu
Cook Time: *45 minutes*   *Servings: 4*
Ingredients:
For Instant Pot Ingredients:
- 1 cup carrot coins
- 1 heaping teaspoon of corn starch
- 1 package firm tofu (14-ounces) cubed
- ¼ cup onions, sliced

For Sauce Ingredients:
- ½ cup water
- 1 teaspoon garlic, minced
- ½ tablespoon rice vinegar
- 3 tablespoons maple syrup
- 3 tablespoons nutritional yeast
- 1 tablespoon ginger, minced
- ¼ cup gluten free soy sauce

For Serving:
Cooked quinoa, brown rice or other grain or lettuce leaves to make fresh wraps, and sesame seeds for garnish.

Directions:
Wrap the block of tofu in paper towels and press for 5 minutes. Remove the paper towels and cut the tofu into ½ inch thick pieces. In a mixing bowl add the sauce ingredients and whisk together.
Set your instant pot to the sauté mode, add the oil and heat it. Add the tofu, carrots, and onions, and brown tofu on all sides, cooking for about 5-minutes. Add the sauce mix to the pot and stir. Close the pot lid and set to Manual mode, on high, with a cook time of 5-minutes. When the cook time is completed, release the pressure using quick-release. Serve with choice of quinoa or brown cooked rice.
Nutritional Information per serving:
Calories: 162   Fat: 0.8g   Carbs: 31g   Protein: 7.1g

Instant Pot Broccoli & Tomato Pasta
Cook Time: *10 minutes*   *Servings: 8*
Ingredients:
- 1 bag of organic Broccoli, frozen (10-ounces)
- 1 box of organic pasta (16-ounces)
- 1 jar of organic tomato, basil pasta sauce (25-ounces)
- 4 quarts of water

Directions:
In a large pot bring the water to boil, and add pasta and stir, cook for 5-minutes. Once pasta is cooked, add in the broccoli and stir. Add the tomato, basil pasta sauce to instant pot and set to Manual setting with a cook time of 5-minutes. Drain the pasta and add it along with

broccoli into instant pot and mix with sauce. Close the lid, when the cook time is completed, release pressure naturally for 10-minutes. Serve hot.

Nutritional Information per serving:
Calories: 262   Fat: 6.2g   Carbs: 42.1g   Protein: 9g

Refried Beans
Cook Time: 28 minutes   **Servings: 4**
Ingredients:
- 1 onion, large, cut into fourths
- 3 cups vegetable broth
- 1 teaspoon chili powder
- ½ cup salsa
- 1 teaspoon paprika
- ½ teaspoon black pepper
- 1 Jalapeno, seeded
- 4 garlic cloves, peeled, chopped roughly
- 1 teaspoon cumin
- 2 cups pinto beans, rinsed well, dried
- Salt to taste

Directions:
Add all ingredients into your instant pot and stir. Close and secure the pot lid and set to Manual setting on high with a cook time of 28-minutes. When the cook time is completed, release the pressure naturally for 10-minutes. Using a high-speed blender blend the beans to get the consistency you want. Serve hot.

Nutritional Information per serving:
Calories: 369   Fat: 1.6g   Carbs: 67.9g   Protein: 22.1g

Peanut & Sweet Potato Stew
Cook Time: 20 minutes   **Servings: 4**
Ingredients:
- 2 cups of kale or another leafy green
- 1 tablespoon ginger, fresh, minced
- 1 teaspoon coriander, dried
- ½ cup peanut butter
- 1 sweet potato, medium, peeled, diced
- ½ teaspoon red chili pepper, crushed
- 1 onion, medium, minced finely
- 3 garlic cloves, finely minced
- 2 cups vegetable broth
- 1 (14.5 ounce) can of tomatoes, diced or crushed
- 1 ½ cups peas frozen or canned
- 1 can black kidney beans, drained and rinsed
- 2 tablespoons olive oil
- Salt and pepper to taste

Directions:
In a food processor or blender, blend the diced tomatoes along with their juice for a few seconds. Set your instant pot to the sauté mode, add oil and heat. Add the onion and cook for 2-minutes. Add the garlic, ginger and chili, and cook for an additional 3-minutes. Add in the tomatoes and stir, then add the peanut butter, coriander while stirring frequently. Add sweet potatoes and broth. Close and lock the pot lid, and set to Manual on high with a cook time of 10-minutes. When the cook time is completed, release the pressure using quick-release. Add the peas, black beans, and greens, and set on sauté mode for 5-minutes, stirring occasionally. Season with salt and pepper. Serve hot.

Nutritional Information per serving:
Calories: 457   Fat: 24.4g   Carbs: 47.8g   Protein: 18.8g

White Bean Stew with Kale & Winter Squash
Cook Time: 25 minutes   **Servings: 6**
Ingredients:

- 1 ½ teaspoons of cumin, ground, divided
- 5 cups water
- 1 bunch of kale, stems removed, sliced
- ½ cup basil, fresh, chopped
- 1 can (15-ounce) tomatoes, diced, fire-roasted
- 1 Jalapeno pepper, seeded, finely chopped
- 1 red bell pepper, large, chopped
- Salt to taste
- 1 onion, large, chopped
- 2 teaspoons oregano, dried, divided
- 1 cup corn, fresh or frozen
- 4 garlic cloves, minced
- 1 lb. navy beans, dried, quick soaked or soaked overnight
- 4 teaspoons smoked paprika, divided
- 1 lb. winter squash, cubed into ¾ dice
- 1 teaspoon basil, dried

Directions:
Set your instant pot to the sauté mode, add oil and heat. Add in onion with a pinch of baking soda, and cook for 2-minutes. Add the garlic and cook for an additional 3-minutes. Add the beans, 1 teaspoon oregano, 2 teaspoons paprika, dried basil, 1 teaspoon cumin and water into instant pot. Close and lock the pot lid and set to Manual on high with a cook time of 8-minutes.
When the cook time is completed, release the pressure using the quick-release. Add the squash and tomatoes to instant pot, along with leftover peppers, seasonings and salt. Close and lock the lid and set to Manual setting for another 8-minutes of cook time. When the cook time is completed, use the quick-release once again. Add in the peas, and kale and stir. Set the pot on sauté for a 5-minute cook time, stirring often. Serve hot.

Nutritional Information per serving:
Calories: 205   Fat: 1.7g   Carbs: 42.3g   Protein: 9.8g

Lasagna Soup
Cook Time: 35 minutes   **Servings: 6**
Ingredients:
For the Pesto Ricotta:

- ¼ lb. extra firm tofu, drained
- 1 tablespoon lemon juice, freshly squeezed
- Pepper and salt to taste

For the Lasagna Soup:

- 1 can (14-ounce) tomatoes, diced
- 3 cups spinach leaves, fresh, chopped
- 4 tablespoons of prepared vegan pesto
- ¼ cup almond milk, unflavored
- 1 cup cashews, raw, soaked in water for 8 hours, drained and rinsed
- 1 teaspoon oregano, dried
- ¾ cup brown lentils, dried

- 1 can (14-ounce) tomatoes, crushed
- 3 cloves garlic, minced
- 1 onion, medium, diced
- 4 ½ cups vegetable broth
- 1 teaspoon basil, dried
- 8 lasagna noodles, broken into pieces

Directions:
In the bottom of your instant pot add onion, broth, basil, garlic, lentils, oregano, and stir to blend. Set to Manual setting with on high with a cook time of 20-minutes. When the cook time is completed, release the pressure naturally for 10-minutes. Add in the crushed tomatoes and stir. Close lid to pot and set on Manual with a cook time of 5-minutes. When the cook time is completed, release the pressure using quick-release. Add in the spinach and noodles and stir. Season with salt and pepper. Set to Manual with a cook time of 10-minutes. Place the soaked cashews and milk into a food processor and blend on high until smooth. Add in the tofu; and pulse a few times, until mix has a ricotta-like texture. Add lemon juice, pesto and season with salt and pepper to taste. Divide the soup into serving bowls, and top each bowl with a dollop of vegan pesto ricotta. Serve warm.

Nutritional Information per serving:
Calories: 300   Fat: 10.3g   Carbs: 40.1g   Protein: 14.7g

Chapter 11. Desserts & Appetizer Instant Pot Recipes

Chocolate Almond Fudge Cake
Cook Time: 2 hours
Servings: 8
Ingredients:
- 1 cup almond flour
- 2 tablespoons Truvia
- ½ cup chocolate almond milk
- 2 tablespoons canola oil
- 2 tablespoons dark cocoa powder
- 2 teaspoons baking soda
- 1 teaspoon vanilla extract
- Pinch of salt
- ½ cup almonds, slivered

Directions:
Mix the Truvia, flour, baking powder, pinch of salt in a mixing bowl. Add the oil, vanilla extract, almond slivers and almond milk, then whisk until smooth. Pour the batter into a greased instant pot. Place the lid on and secure, then set to Manual on high for a 2-hour cook time using the slow cooking feature. Once the cook time is completed, release the pressure naturally for 15-minutes. Remove the lid and allow the cake to cool completely. Garnish the cake with chocolate sauce and whipped cream.

Nutritional Information per serving:
Calories: 322   Fats: 3g   Carbs: 19g   Proteins: 4g

Pumpkin Chocolate Chip Bundt Cake
Cook Time: 35 minutes
Servings: 8
Ingredients:
- ¾ cup unbleached all-purpose flour
- ¾ cup whole wheat flour
- ½ a can (15-ounce) of 100% pureed pumpkin
- 1 teaspoon baking soda
- 2 tablespoons canola oil
- ½ cup 2% Greek yogurt
- 2 tablespoons Truvia or ¾ cup sugar
- 1 medium banana, mashed
- ½ teaspoon baking powder
- ¾ teaspoon pumpkin pie spice
- ½ teaspoon salt
- 1 egg
- ½ teaspoon pure vanilla extract
- 2/3 cup semi-sweet chocolate chips
- 1.5 cups of water for instant pot

Directions:
In a mixing bowl combine, salt, baking soda, flour, baking powder, pumpkin pie spice and set aside. Using an electric mixer to combine Truvia, yogurt, oil, banana, pureed pumpkin, egg and vanilla extract (in a separate bowl from dry ingredients). With the mixer on low, gradually add the dry ingredients. Fold in the chocolate chips.
Grease the pan or use cooking spray, and transfer the batter to the bundt pan. Add water into the inner stainless steel pot, and place the trivet inside. Place the bundt pan on top of trivet, and close the lid and lock it. Press the Manual mode and set for a cook time of 35-minutes. When the cook time is completed, release the pressure naturally for 10-minutes. Allow the pan to cool before trying to remove it.

Nutritional Information per serving:
Calories: 356   Fats: 4g   Carbs: 22g   Proteins: 7g

Tapioca Pudding
Cook Time: 7 minutes
Servings: 6
Ingredients:
- 3 cups milk
- 2 tablespoons Truvia or ½ cup sugar
- 4 tablespoons tapioca
- 1 teaspoon vanilla extract
- 1 egg

Directions:
Spray the inside of your instant pot with non-stick cooking spray. Add all ingredients except the egg, and stir well. Place the lid on your instant pot and set to Manual for a cook time of 7-minutes. When the cook time is completed, release the pressure naturally for 10-minutes. Lightly beat the egg in a bowl. Once the tapioca starts to bubble in the pot stir and temper the egg by adding a spoonful of the tapioca mixture to the egg. Add the tempered egg slowly to the pudding and stir until fully integrated. Eat warm or chill to serve cold.

Nutritional Information per serving:
Calories: 272   Fats: 2g   Carbs: 20g   Proteins: 5g

Carrot Cake
Cook Time: 32 minutes
Servings: 8
Ingredients:
- 2 eggs
- 1 ½ cups shredded carrots
- 2/3 cup vegetable oil
- ½ teaspoon nutmeg
- ½ teaspoon salt
- ½ teaspoon baking soda
- 1 teaspoon baking powder
- 2 tablespoons Truvia or 1 cup sugar
- 1 cup flour
- ½ cup water for instant pot

Directions:
In a large mixing bowl combine, carrots, oil, sugar (or Truvia), and eggs together. In another bowl mix the dry ingredients. Fold the wet ingredients into dry, mixing until just wet. Spray a 6-inch springform pan with cooking spray and pour in the batter. Pour ½ cup water into instant pot, place in the trivet, and place pan on top of trivet. Set to Manual setting for a cook time of 35-minutes. When cook time is completed, release the pressure naturally for 10-minutes. Serve.

Nutritional Information per serving:
Calories: 274   Fats: 3g   Carbs: 21g   Proteins: 18g

Brownies
Cook Time: 18 minutes **Servings: 8**
Ingredients:
- ¼ cup cocoa powder
- ½ cup almond flour
- 1 teaspoon vanilla extract
- 3 eggs
- ¼ cup brown sugar
- 2 tablespoons Truvia, or ½ cup white sugar
- 2 tablespoons chocolate chips
- 4 tablespoons unsalted butter
- 1 cup water for instant pot

Directions:
Melt the chocolate and butter together in the microwave. Beat the butter/chocolate mixture together with sugars until well combined. Add the eggs one at a time, add vanilla while beating. Sift flour, cocoa over the wet ingredients and stir to combine. Add 1 cup of water into instant pot, add the trivet. Add batter to ramekins, and place them on top of trivet. Close the instant pot lid, and set to Manual mode with a cook time of 18-minutes. When the cook time is competed, release the pressure naturally for 15-minutes. Serve.

Nutritional Information per serving:
Calories: 312   Fats: 2g   Carbs: 24g   Proteins: 21g

Apple Crisp
Cook Time: 8 minutes   **Servings: 8**
Ingredients:
- 5 medium Granny Smith apples
- 2 teaspoons cinnamon
- ¼ brown sugar
- ¼ cup almond flour
- ¾ cup old fashioned rolled oats
- 4 tablespoons butter
- ½ cup water
- ½ teaspoon nutmeg
- ½ teaspoon salt

Directions:
Peel, core, and dice granny smith apples. Insert the apples on the bottom of your instant pot. Sprinkle with cinnamon and nutmeg. Top with water. In a bowl melt butter, add oats, flour, brown sugar and salt and mix. Drop the crumble mix by the spoonful into your instant pot on top of apples. Close and secure the instant pot lid, set to Manual setting for a cook time on high of 8-minutes. When the cook time is completed, release the pressure naturally for 10-minutes. Serve warm.

Nutritional Information per serving:
Calories: 314   Fats: 4g   Carbs: 23g   Proteins: 8g

Vanilla Fruit Cake
Cook Time: 20 minutes   **Servings: 6**
Ingredients:
- 10-ounces fruit
- 2 eggs

- Powdered sugar
- 1 tablespoon olive oil
- 1 teaspoon vanilla extract
- 1 cup milk
- 7 tablespoons almond flour
- 4 tablespoons sugar, or 2 tablespoons Truvia
- 2 cups water for instant pot

Directions:
Add the trivet and 2 cups of water to your instant pot. Wash and prepare the fruit of your choice. In a mixing bowl, add eggs, sugar, vanilla and mix them well with a whisk or a fork. Next add the milk and flour. Oil the form and line with wax paper. Pour the mixture, and then sprinkle the fruit into mixture. Cover tightly with tin foil. Place on trivet, and set on Manual mode, with a cook time of 20-minutes. When the cook time is completed, release the pressure naturally for 10-minutes. Allow to cool, then transfer to serving dishes, sprinkle with powdered sugar right before serving.

Nutritional Information per serving:
Calories: 343   Fats: 3g   Carbs: 25g   Proteins: 19g

Creamy Chocolate Cheesecake
Cook Time: 45 minutes   **Servings: 8**
Ingredients:
- 8-ounces cream cheese
- 4-ounces milk chocolate
- 1 cup sugar or 3 tablespoons Truvia
- 4-ounces white chocolate
- 4-ounces dark chocolate
- 1 ½ teaspoons vanilla extract
- ½ cup plain Greek yogurt
- 3 large eggs
- 1 tablespoon cornstarch
- 1 cup sugar or 3 tablespoons Truvia

Directions:
Take a 7-inch springform pan and spray with non-stick cooking spray. Use parchment paper to line the bottom of the pan. In mixing bowl, mix cookie crumbs and melted butter and press straight to the bottom of the pan. Store in the freezer to set for a day. Blend the cream cheese with a handheld mixer until smooth. Add the sugar and cornstarch, while mixing on low speed, do this until well combined. Add the eggs to mixture, one at a time, continuing to beat and scrape the bowl. Add yogurt and vanilla, mixing until well combined. Divide your batter into three separate bowls (about 2 cups each).

In the microwave, melt your milk chocolate for 30 seconds, stir. Return chocolate to the microwave for an additional 30 seconds, stir until completely melted and smooth. Whisk it into one of the bowls of cheesecake batter. Repeat this process with the white and dark chocolate (each being mixed in a different bowl of dough). Store the bowls in the fridge for about 20-minutes so they will be firmer for layering. Remove the bowls from the fridge and remove the pan, with the crust out of freezer.

Add the dark chocolate batter into center of the crust, making sure to smooth, to form an even layer. Carefully spoon dollops of your white chocolate mixture on top of the dark chocolate, carefully smoothing over the top. Repeat process with the milk chocolate mixture. Add 1 cup of water to your instant pot, placing the trivet inside it. Place the cake pan on top of trivet, and set to Manual setting on high for a cook time of 45-minutes. When the cook time is completed, release the pressure naturally for 15-minutes. Carefully remove the cake pan from your instant pot. Allow the cake to cool completely and then cover with plastic wrap, and place it in the fridge overnight.

Before serving allow the cake to stand at room temperature for an hour or so. To make the cake look even more pleasing to the eye, decorate the cake with sugared cranberries, if desired.

Nutritional Information per serving:
Calories: 358   Fats: 4g   Carbs: 28g   Proteins: 24g

Apple Crumb Cake
Cook Time: 20 minutes   *Servings: 8*
Ingredients:
- ¼ cup raw sugar
- 6-ounces butter
- 2 tablespoons all-purpose flour
- 6 small apples
- 2 tablespoons all-purpose flour

Crumb filling:
- 5 teaspoons cinnamon
- 5 tablespoons sugar or 2 tablespoons Truvia
- 5-ounces dry breadcrumbs
- ½ a lemon's juice and rind
- 1 tablespoon ginger powder

Directions:
Prepare the crumb filling by combining the breadcrumbs, lemon juice, ginger, cinnamon, sugar, lemon zest and melted butter. Mix the ingredients well and set aside. Take your unpeeled washed apple, make sure to remove their cores. Then, slice them very thinly, using a mandolin, if you can. Butter the interior of your container all the way around the edge of it. Add the flour to the container and swoosh the flour around so it will evenly coat container. Start layering your apple slices. The bottom of your cake will become the top when you flip the cake out of the container. So, arrange apple slices carefully for the first layer of your cake. Add a layer of breadcrumb mixture to it.

Alternate apple and breadcrumb layers until you have filled your container. Once you have finished filling your bowl, cover tightly with tin foil. Add 1 cup of water to your instant pot, also and the trivet inside your instant pot. Place the container on top of the trivet, set to Manual on high for a cook time of 20-minutes. When the cook time is completed, release the pressure naturally for 10-minutes. Sprinkle the top of cake with a layer of raw sugar and grill until the sugar has melted and the top of the cake has a nice golden brown color to it.

Nutritional Information per serving:
Calories: 258   Fats: 1g   Carbs: 8g   Proteins: 5g

Raspberry Cream Cheesecake
Cook Time: 25 minutes   *Servings: 8*
Ingredients:
- 28g butter, melted
- 12 crushed Oreo cookie crumbs

Filling:

- 2 eggs
- 1 tablespoon all-purpose flour
- ¼ cup sour cream

Topping:
- Fresh raspberries
- 3 ½ ounces milk chocolate

- ¼ cup sugar
- 16-ounces cream cheese
- ½ cup seedless raspberry jam
- 1/3 cup heavy cream

Directions:
Begin by preparing a 7-inch springform pan, and coating it with a non-stick spray. You can also line it with parchment paper if desired. Combine Oreo cookie crumbs and butter in a mixing bowl. Spread mixture, evenly on the bottom and 1-inch up the side of pan. Store in the freezer for at least 10-minutes. In a mixing bowl, mix cream cheese, and sugar at medium speed with blender until smooth. Blend in the jam, sour cream, and flour. Mix in the eggs, one at a time, until mixture is well combined. Add the batter into the springform pan on top of the crust.

Add 1 cup of water into instant pot and place trivet inside. Place the cake pan on top of trivet, and close lid of pot. Set to Manual setting on high for a cook time of 25-minutes. When the cook time is completed, release the pressure naturally for 15-minutes. Carefully remove the cheesecake from your instant pot. Place the springform pan on a wire rack to cool. Once the cheesecake has cooled, cover it with plastic wrap and place in the fridge for at least 4 hours or overnight. When the cheesecake is cooled, prepare topping, place half of the chocolate into a mixing bowl. Heat your heavy cream over medium-high heat until it reaches a boil. Remove the cream from heat, and pour the cream over chocolate and stir until chocolate is fully melted. Add the remaining chocolate and stir until it has all melted and well combined. Allow it to cool until it has thickened enough to drip down the sides of the cheesecake. Drizzle the chocolate over top of the cheesecake. Decorate the top of cake with fresh raspberries, to add to the taste and look of this yummy treat. Keep cake refrigerated until ready to serve.

Nutritional Information per serving:
Calories: 318   Fats: 4g   Carbs: 21g   Proteins: 19g

Crema Catalana
Cook Time: 13 minutes   **Servings: 4**

Ingredients:
- 1 stick of cinnamon
- 1 orange zested
- 3 tablespoons white sugar

Garnish:
- 1 teaspoon nutmeg

- 6 egg yolks
- 18-ounces fresh cream

- 2 tablespoons raw sugar for caramelizing

Directions:
Begin with heating up the citrus zest, cream, cinnamon in a small saucepan over low heat, and stirring occasionally. Once the cream begins to boil, turn off the heat, allow it to infuse for 30-minutes. In the meantime, add 2 cups of water to your instant pot, and place the

steamer basket inside of instant pot. Set aside. In a small mixing bowl, add egg yolks, sugar, and whisk until the sugar is dissolved. Once the cream has cooled to room temperature, add the yolks and whisk, just enough to mix ingredients well. Pour the mixture slowly through a strainer into a spouted container. Put the mixture into ramekins, cover tightly with foil and place them into steamer basket. Close and secure the lid of your instant pot. Set it to Manual mode with a cook time of 8-minutes. When the cook time has completed, release the pressure naturally for 10-minutes.

Remove the custards from your instant pot, and allow them to cool on a wire rack. Cover custards with some plastic wrap and keep them in the fridge for 4-hours to chill. Before serving custards, grate some nutmeg over top of them, and sprinkle a layer of sugar over them as well. Serve warm or cold.

Nutritional Information per serving:
Calories: 302   Fats: 3g   Carbs: 23g   Proteins: 22g

Cranberry Cake
Cook Time: 50 minutes　　　　　　　　　**Servings: 10**
Ingredients:

- 3 ½ ounces apricots, dry
- 3 ½ ounces of cranberries, dry
- 1 teaspoon olive oil
- 8 tablespoons sugar or 3 tablespoons Truvia
- 2 teaspoons baking powder
- 1 teaspoon ginger
- 3 ½ ounces carrot, grated
- 2-ounces maple syrup (can use sugar-free syrup)
- 4 large eggs
- 7-ounces butter
- Pinch of salt
- 1 teaspoon cinnamon

Directions:
Add dried apricots and cranberries into a deep bowl, cover them with boiling water. Prepare a pudding mold, by adding a drop of olive oil, then spreading it around with a paper towel until the inside of the bowl is well covered, then set mold aside. Add 2 cups of water to your instant pot, also place the trivet inside of your instant pot.

Add the sugar, flour, baking powder, ginger, cinnamon, and salt into a food processor. Pulse a few times to mix the mixture. Add chopped butter, and pulse a few more times. Add the eggs and maple syrup, and pulse a few times until well blended. Strain dried food and rinse it under cold water. Now, lightly sprinkle the dried fruit and grated carrot on top of the mixture. Add to the prepared bowl, your pudding batter. Place the uncovered bowl onto top of trivet. Close and secure the lid to the instant pot. Set to the Brown/Sauté setting, when the steam starts to come out of the instant pot (in about 10-minutes), start counting down 15-minutes of steam without the pre-cooking time. Set your instant pot to Manual on high with a cook time of 35-minutes. When the cook time is completed, release the pressure naturally for 15-minutes. Remove the pudding from your instant pot and cover it tightly, until ready to invert and serve. Just before serving, give it a dousing of fresh cream.

Chocoflan

Cook Time: 20 minutes **Servings:** 8

Ingredients:

For Caramel:
- 1 cup sugar
- 2 tablespoons butter
- 1 teaspoon vanilla extract
- 2 tablespoons heavy cream
- ¼ cup corn syrup

For Flan:
- 1 cup whole milk
- 2 eggs
- 1 cup condensed milk
- 1 teaspoon vanilla extract

For Cake:
- 7 tablespoons almond flour
- 6 tablespoons sugar or 2 tablespoons Truvia
- 1 ½ tablespoons cocoa powder
- 8 tablespoons yogurt
- 2 tablespoons olive oil
- 1 egg
- 1/3 teaspoon salt
- ½ teaspoon baking powder
- ½ teaspoon baking soda

Directions:

Add 2 cups of water to your instant pot, and place the trivet inside of it. Prepare the caramel by heating all ingredients in a small saucepan over low heat. Stir often, and when it begins to boil remove from heat, and pour into tube pan. In a mixing bowl, make the flan by breaking up the eggs well using a fork, mix in the milk, sweetened condensed milk, and vanilla. In another mixing bowl, mix all the dry ingredients for the cake. Add the cocoa, flour, sugar, baking soda, baking powder and salt, mix well. Using a small bowl, break up the egg mix in the oil and yogurt. Scrape out all the yogurt and egg from small bowl using a spatula. Combine this mix with flour/cocoa mixture using a fork to mix until well combined. Spatula out the chocolate cake mixture into the caramel-coated tube pan, and flatten into a flat layer. Pour the flan mixture on top of that. Set the tube pan in the middle of a foil sling and lower it on top of trivet. Close and secure lid to instant pot, and set to Manual on high with a cook time of 20-minutes. When the cook time is completed, release the pressure naturally for 15-minutes. Lift the dessert out of instant pot and allow it to cool. Cover it with plastic wrap and place in the fridge overnight. Top with upside down serving plate and quickly flip. Remove the tube pan from the cake and serve with an optional sprinkling of pecans or ground pistachios.

Nutritional Information per serving:
Calories: 326 Fats: 2g Carbs: 26g Proteins: 32g

Cheese Flan Cake
Cook Time: 15 minutes **Servings:** 10
Ingredients:
- 1 teaspoon nutmeg
- Caramel: 4 tablespoons sugar
- 1 teaspoon cinnamon
- 1 teaspoon vanilla extract
- 5 eggs
- 8-ounces cream cheese
- 1 ½ cups evaporated milk
- 2 cups sweetened condensed milk

Directions:
Make caramel; use your flan pan to melt sugar. Stir until melted and is medium brown in color. Remove from heat and swirl the liquid sugar to coat the sides of the pan. Allow it cool, meanwhile make custard. Put the cream cheese in a mixing bowl. Add one egg at a time until well blended. Add the remaining ingredients and then add to your caramelized pan. Add a cup of water into instant pot, and place trivet inside of it. Place the pan on top of trivet, and set on Manual mode with a cook time of 15-minutes. When the cook time is completed, naturally release the pressure for 15-minutes. Remove the flan and allow it to cool to room temperature, then place it in fridge overnight. Run a knife around the edge of the pan, flip onto a plate that has a rim to catch caramel. Slice and serve!

Nutritional Information per serving:
Calories: 357   Fats: 5g   Carbs: 25g   Proteins: 37g

Raspberry Curd
Cook Time: 5 minutes **Servings:** 4
Ingredients:
- 4 egg yolks
- 24-ounces raspberries
- 4 tablespoons butter
- 4 tablespoons lemon juice
- 2 cups sugar or 2 tablespoons Truvia

Directions:
Add the raspberries, sugar, lemon juice into your instant pot and stir. Cover and cook on the Manual setting with a cook time of 1-minute. When the cook time is completed, release the pressure using the quick-release. Strain the contents through a fine wire mesh strainer and discard the seeds. Whisk the yolks. Add the strained raspberry pulp into the yolks and whisk. Pour into instant pot and sauté for 5-minutes, stirring constantly. Add butter and turn off pot. Pour into serving bowls and chill for a couple of hours before serving.

Nutritional Information per serving:
Calories: 224   Fat: 1.2g   Carbs: 32g   Protein: 6.4g

Fruit Clafoutis Cake
Cook Time: 20 minutes
Servings: 8
Ingredients:

- 5 cups fruits, of your choice, chopped
- 1 ½ cups sugar or 2 tablespoons Truvia
- 4 medium eggs
- 1 ½ cups all-purpose flour
- 2 tablespoons vanilla extract
- 2 cups milk

Directions:
Whisk the eggs, sugar, and vanilla together in a mixing bowl. Add the flour and milk and whisk well until smooth. Grease a heatproof dish and line it with parchment paper. Pour the batter into the dish. Sprinkle the assorted chopped fruit over the top of mixture. Cover with foil. Place a trivet into your instant pot, and pour 2 cups of water into pot. Place the dish with mixture on top of trivet. Close the pot lid, and select Manual setting on high with a cook time of 20-minutes. When the cook time is completed, release the pressure naturally for 10-minutes. Remove the dish from instant pot and allow it to sit for awhile. Sprinkle powdered sugar over it just before serving. Serve warm or chilled.

Nutritional Information per serving:
Calories: 272   Fat: 1.5g   Carbs: 38g   Protein: 5.2g

Yams Citrus
Cook Time: 7 minutes
Servings: 2
Ingredients:

- 2 yams, halved
- ¼ teaspoon salt
- 1 tablespoon butter
- ¾ cup brown sugar or to taste
- 1 ½ tablespoons orange zest, grated
- 1 cup orange juice

Directions:
Set the yams facing up on the bottom of your instant pot. Pour in the orange juice. Sprinkle yams with salt and half the orange zest. Sprinkle yams with brown sugar. Close the lid, and select Manual setting on high with a cook time of 7-minutes. When the cook time is completed, release the pressure using the quick-release. Mash the yams with a potato masher. Add butter, more brown sugar is desired, and remaining orange zest. Serve warm.

Nutritional Information per serving:
Calories: 243   Fat: 1.0g   Carbs: 27g   Protein: 5.1g

Chocolate Custard
Cook Time: 35 minutes **Servings: 8**
Ingredients:
- 9 egg yolks, whisked
- 3 cups dark cooking chocolate, finely chopped
- ¾ cup castor sugar
- 1 ½ teaspoons vanilla extract
- 2 cups full fat milk
- Fresh strawberries for garnish
- 1 ½ cups cream

Directions:
Pour 2 cups of water into your instant pot, and place the trivet inside of it. Pour cream, milk, vanilla and sugar into a saucepan. Place the saucepan over medium heat, and simmer until the sugar is dissolved. Remove from heat and add chocolate pieces and stir until the chocolate melts. Gently pour the yolks into the mixture while whisking. Pour the mixture into a heatproof dish and place on top of the trivet. Close the lid on pot, and select the Manual setting on high with a cook time of 30-minutes. When the cook time is completed, release the pressure naturally for 10-minutes. Remove the dish from pot and allow it to sit for awhile. Serve warm and garnish with strawberries.

Nutritional Information per serving:
Calories: 282   Fat: 1.4g   Carbs: 37g   Protein: 5.3g

Bread Pudding
Cook Time: 10 minutes **Servings: 8**
Ingredients:
- 8 slices old bread, trim crusts, cut into cubes
- 4 eggs, lightly beaten
- 4 cups warm milk
- 1 cup walnuts, chopped
- 1 teaspoon cinnamon + extra for garnish
- 1 cup golden raisins
- ½ teaspoon salt
- 2 tablespoons butter
- 1 cup, light brown sugar
- Zest of an orange, cut into thin strips
- 1 teaspoon vanilla extract
- 3 cups water

Directions:
Grease heatproof dish with butter, then set it aside. In a mixing bowl, mix bread, walnuts, raisins, and orange zest. In a separate mixing bowl, mix brown sugar, cinnamon, eggs, salt, milk, and vanilla extract. Pour this mixture into the bowl of bread mix. Mix well, then transfer bread mixture into the prepared dish. Cover dish with foil. Pour water into instant pot, and place the trivet in. Set the dish on top of the trivet, and close lid to pot. Set on Manual setting on high with cook time of 10-minutes. When the cooking is completed, release the pressure naturally for 10-minutes. Remove the dish from instant pot and loosen the foil and allow it to cool a bit. Sprinkle with cinnamon for garnish, and serve warm.

Nutritional Information per serving:
Calories: 289   Fat: 2.4g   Carbs: 31g   Protein: 6.1g

Blueberry Custard
Cook Time: 25 minutes
Servings: 4
Ingredients:
- 4 eggs
- 1 ½ tablespoons confectioners' sugar
- ½ teaspoon nutmeg, ground
- ½ cup blueberries
- 1/3 cup almond flour
- 2 tablespoons honey
- 1 ½ tablespoons butter, melted
- 1 ¼ cups milk
- ½ teaspoon vanilla extract
- ¼ teaspoon salt

Directions:
Add the butter to a baking dish and spread the butter all over the dish. Blend the honey, milk, vanilla, flour, salt, and eggs until smooth. Pour into dish. Sprinkle the blueberries all over mix. Place trivet inside of instant pot, along with 2 cups of water. Place the dish on top of trivet. Close lid and select Manual setting on high with a cook time of 25-minutes. When the cook time is completed, release the pressure naturally for 15-minutes. Chill for a few hours. When ready to serve, run a knife all around the edges of the pan and invert on to a plate. Sprinkle nutmeg and confectioners' sugar for garnish and serve chilled.

Nutritional Information per serving:
Calories: 304 Fat: 2.3g Carbs: 38g Protein: 7.2g

Purple Pudding
Cook Time: 5 minutes
Servings: 6
Ingredients:
- 2 cans thick coconut cream, divided
- 5 cups water
- ½ cup brown sugar
- ½ cup seed tapioca
- 1 cup ripe jackfruit, cubed
- 1 cup glutinous rice, shaped into balls
- 1 cup taro root, cubed
- 2 cups ripe plantains, sliced into disks
- 1 ½ cups purple yam, cubed

Directions:
Add the purple yam, glutinous rice, taro root, ripe plantains, ripe jackfruit, brown sugar, tapioca pearls, and water into instant pot. Close the lid and set to Manual setting on high for a cook time of 5-minutes. When the cook time is completed, release the pressure using the quick-release. Add the coconut cream, and allow the residual heat to cook the cream. Serve by ladling pudding into bowls. Serve cold.

Nutritional Information per serving:
Calories: 262 Fat: 1.3g Carbs: 27g Protein: 6.5g

Mango & Cashew Cake
Cook Time: 35 minutes **Servings:** 8
Ingredients:
- ½ cup powdered sugar for dusting top of cake
- ¼ cup cashew nuts, ground
- ¼ cup mango jam
- ½ cup cashew milk
- 1 teaspoon vanilla essence
- ½ teaspoon baking soda
- ¼ cup coconut butter
- ½ cup almond flour
- 2 cups of water for instant pot
- 1 teaspoon baking powder

Directions:
Lightly grease bundt pan with coconut oil, and dust pan with flour. Set aside. In a mixing bowl, mix coconut butter, almond flour, baking powder, baking soda, vanilla essence, milk, and mango jam. Stir well to combine. Pour the batter into the bundt pan. Add 2 cups of water to your instant pot, add in the trivet, and place the bundt pan on top of trivet. Close the lid to pot, and set to Manual setting on high for a cook time of 35-minutes. When the cook time is completed, release the pressure naturally for 15-minutes. Transfer the bundt cake onto a rack and allow to cool at room temperature. Place on a platter, sprinkle with ground cashews and powdered sugar. Slice and serve at room temperature.

Nutritional Information per serving:
Calories: 293   Fat: 1.2g   Carbs: 29g   Protein: 6.8g

Corn Pudding
Cook Time: 2 minutes **Servings:** 4
Ingredients:
- 1 can cream of corn
- ¾ cup rice
- ¼ cup white sugar or 1 tablespoon Truvia
- 3 cups water
- Pinch of salt
- 2 cans thick coconut cream
- ¼ cup freshly toasted coconut flakes, for garnish

Directions:
Add the rice, cream of corn, salt, white sugar, and water into your instant pot. Stir well to blend. Close the lid to pot, and select Manual setting on high for a cook time of 2-minutes. When the cook time is completed, release the pressure using the quick-release. Add in the coconut cream and stir. Ladle into bowls and garnish with coconut flakes. Serve cold.

Nutritional Information per serving:
Calories: 282   Fat: 1.4g   Carbs: 24g   Protein: 5.1g

Pumpkin Pie
Cook Time: 35 minutes **Servings:** 8
Ingredients:
Crust:

- ½ cup crushed pecan sandies cookies, about 6 cookies
- 1/3 cup toasted pecans, chopped
- 2 tablespoons butter, melted

Filling:
- ½ teaspoon salt
- ½ cup light brown sugar
- 1 ½ teaspoon pumpkin pie spice
- 2 tablespoons lemon zest
- 1 ½ cups oats
- 1 ½ cups light brown sugar
- 1 ¼ cups almond flour
- ½ cup evaporated milk
- 1 ½ cups pumpkin puree
- 1 egg beaten
- 1 teaspoon cinnamon, ground
- 1 teaspoon nutmeg, ground
- 1 ½ sticks butter

Directions:
Coat a 7-inch spring-form pan with non-stick cooking spray. In a mixing bowl, combine pecans, cookie crumbs, butter (melted), and spread evenly over pan bottom. Set in the freezer for about 10-minutes. In another mixing bowl, add brown sugar, pumpkin pie spice, salt, egg, pumpkin puree, evaporated milk and mix well. Pour mix onto pie crust and cover with foil. Pour 1 cup of water into bottom of instant pot, and set trivet inside. Take an 18-inch long piece of foil and fold it over twice. Carefully place the pan onto the foil strip, and lower in onto the trivet, fold the foil so you can close the instant pot lid. Close the lid, and select the Manual setting on high for a cook time of 35-minutes. When the cook time is completed, release the pressure naturally for 15-minutes. Remove the pan to cool, and remove the foil. When it has cooled, cover the pie with plastic wrap and place in the fridge for at least 4-hours. Serve cold or warm.

Nutritional Information per serving:
Calories: 294   Fat: 1.6g   Carbs: 31g   Protein: 8.3g

Instant Pot Chocolate Fondue

Cook Time: 1 minute
Servings: 8
Ingredients:
- 2 cups of water for instant pot
- 3 ½ ounces dark chocolate 70% cocoa, cut into chunks
- 1 teaspoon sugar or ½ teaspoon Truvia
- Fresh fruit of your choice for serving
- 1 teaspoon Amaretto liquor (optional)
- 3 ½ ounces fresh cream

Directions:
Add 2 cups of water into your instant pot, also place the trivet inside of pot. In a small ceramic fondue pot, or any heat-proof container, place large chunks of chocolate into it. Add the sugar along with the liquor. Carefully, place the container on top of trivet, and close the lid to pot. Select Manual setting on high for a cook time of 1-minute. When the cook time is completed, release the pressure using quick-release. Stir the contents of your mixture until smooth. Using an oven mitt remove container from instant pot. Move to fondue stand with flame on medium setting. Serve fondue with small pieces of your favorite fruits.

Conclusion

I do hope that you have enjoyed reading my recipe book, as much as I have enjoyed writing it. I hope that my recipe collection will offer you some new and healthy options to add to your daily diet.

The best thing that I discovered while writing this book is that your meals do not have to be tasteless and boring to be healthy. Within these pages is a wide selection of recipes that are full of wonderful flavors that will have your tastebuds tingling with delight while at the same time offering you good nutritious meals.

To further reduce your sugar intake, I would suggest replacing any sugars in my recipe collection with the wonderful "Truvia" a calorie-free natural sweetener that comes from the Stevia plant, native to South America. I wish you immense success in adding new and healthier meal choices to your diet—that are not only good for you but taste amazing!

CPSIA information can be obtained
at www.ICGtesting.com
Printed in the USA
BVHW09s1346141018
530044BV00001B/1/P